GOD'S FINAL ENVOY

Studying the Historical Jesus

It was once fashionable to claim that Jesus could not be known as a figure of history and that even if he could be known in that way the result would not be of interest for faith. Both contentions have been laid to rest over the past twenty years.

Scholarship has seen archaeological discoveries, advances in the study of Jewish and Hellenistic literature, a renewed interest in the social milieu of Judaism and Christianity, and critical investigation of the systematic relationship between those two religions (and others in the ancient world). In the midst of these discussions — and many others — Jesus has appeared again and again as a person who can be understood historically and who must be assessed before we can give any complete explanation of the history of the period in which he lived. As he and his movement are better understood, the nature of the faith that they pioneered has been more clearly defined.

Of course, the Jesus who is under investigation cannot simply be equated with whatever the Gospels say of him. The Gospels, composed in Greek a generation after Jesus' death, reflect the faith of early Christians who came to believe in him. Their belief included reference to historical data, but also included the interpretation of Jesus as it had developed after his time.

The critical tasks of coming to grips with the development of the New Testament, the nature of primitive Christian faith, and the historical profile of Jesus are all interrelated. The purpose of this series is to explore key questions concerning Jesus in recent discussion. Each author has already made an important contribution to the study of Jesus and writes for the series on the basis of expertise in the area addressed by his or her particular volume.

Of the many studies of Jesus that are available today, some are suspect in their treatment of primary sources and some do not engage the secondary literature appropriately. **Studying the Historical Jesus** is a series of contributions that are no less sound for being creative. Jesus is a figure of history as well as the focus of Christian theology: discussion of him should be accessible, rigorous, and interesting.

BRUCE CHILTON
Bard College

CRAIG A. EVANS
Trinity Western University

God's Final Envoy

*Early Christology and Jesus'
Own View of His Mission*

Marinus de Jonge

WILLIAM B. EERDMANS PUBLISHING COMPANY
GRAND RAPIDS, MICHIGAN / CAMBRIDGE, U.K.

© 1998 Wm. B. Eerdmans Publishing Co.
255 Jefferson Ave. S.E., Grand Rapids, Michigan 49503 /
P.O. Box 163, Cambridge CB3 9PU U.K.

Printed in the United States of America

03 02 01 00 99 98   7 6 5 4 3 2 1

Library of Congress Cataloging-in-Publication Data

Jonge, Marinus de, 1925-
God's final envoy : early Christology and Jesus' own view of his mission /
M. de Jonge.
        p.   cm.   —   (Studying the historical Jesus)
Includes bibliographical references and index.
ISBN 0-8028-4482-0 (pbk. : alk. paper)
1. Jesus Christ — History of doctrines — Early church, ca. 30-600.
2. Jesus Christ — Person and offices — Biblical teaching.
3. Bible. N.T. — Criticism, interpretation, etc.
I. Title. II. Series.
BT198.J643 1998
232'.09'015 — dc21   98-25620
                                                   CIP

Some of the material in this volume has been adapted from other publications by the author. The author and publisher gratefully acknowledge permission to reuse the material listed on page 151 in this book.

Contents

Abbreviations

AGJU	Arbeiten zur Geschichte des antiken Judentums und des Urchristentums
Ant.	Josephus, *Antiquities of the Jews*
2 Apoc. Bar.	Syriac *Apocalypse of Baruch*
Apoc. Zeph.	*Apocalypse of Zephaniah*
1 Apol.	Justin Martyr, *First Apology*
As. Mos.	*Assumption of Moses*
BBET	Beiträge zur biblischen Exegese und Theologie
B.C.E.	Before the Common Era
BETL	Bibliotheca Ephemeridum Theologicarum Lovaniensium
BHS	Biblia Hebraica Stuttgartensia
Bib	*Biblica*
BZ	*Biblische Zeitschrift*
BZNW	Beihefte zur *Zeitschrift für die Neutestamentliche Wissenschaft*
C.E.	Common Era
ConBNT	Coniectanea Biblica, New Testament
Dial.	Justin Martyr, *Dialogue with Trypho the Jew*
Ebib	Etudes Bibliques
EKK	Evangelisch-katholischer Kommentar
FRLANT	Forschungen zur Religion und Literatur des Alten und Neuen Testaments
HDR	Harvard Dissertations in Religion
HTR	*Harvard Theological Review*

HTKNT	Herders theologischer Kommentar zum Neuen Testament
HTS	Harvard Theological Studies
JBL	*Journal of Biblical Literature*
JJS	*Journal of Jewish Studies*
Jos. As.	*Joseph and Aseneth*
JSJ	*Journal for the Study of Judaism*
JSJSup	Journal for the Study of Judaism — Supplement Series
JSNTSup	Journal for the Study of the New Testament — Supplement Series
Jub.	*Jubilees*
J. W.	Josephus, *The Jewish War*
LXX	Septuagint
1 Macc.	1 Maccabees
2 Macc.	2 Maccabees
NovT	*Novum Testamentum*
NovTSup	Novum Testamentum, Supplements
NTAbh	Neutestamentliche Abhandlungen
NTS	*New Testament Studies*
NTTS	New Testament Tools and Studies
OBO	Orbis Biblicus et Orientalis
OrChr	*Oriens Christianus*
par.	parallel in the Synoptic Gospels
Ps(s). Sol.	*Psalm(s) of Solomon*
QD	Quaestiones Disputatae
1QM	*War Rule* from Qumran Cave 1
11QPs^a	*Psalms Scroll* from Qumran Cave 11
1QS	*Community Rule* from Qumran Cave 1
1QSa	Appendix A *(Rule of the Congregation)* to 1QS
4QWFlor	*Florilegium* from Qumran Cave 4
11QMelch	*Melchizedek* text from Qumran Cave 11
REB	Revised English Bible
SBLMS	Society of Biblical Literature Monograph Series
SBLSBS	Society of Biblical Literature Sources for Biblical Study
SBLSCS	Society of Biblical Literature Septuagint and Cognate Studies
SBS	Stuttgarter Bibelstudien

Sib. Or.	*Sibylline Oracles*
SJLA	Studies in Judaism in Late Antiquity
SJT	*Scottish Journal of Theology*
SNT	Studien zum Neuen Testament
SNTSMS	Society for New Testament Studies Monograph Series
SPB	Studia Postbiblica
SVTP	Studia in Veteris Testamenti Pseudepigrapha
TDNT	G. Kittel and G. Friedrich, eds., *Theological Dictionary of the New Testament*
TU	Texte und Untersuchungen
TWNT	G. Kittel and G. Friedrich, eds., *Theologisches Wörterbuch zum Neuen Testament*
TynBul	*Tyndale Bulletin*
v(v).	verse(s)
VCSup	Vigiliae Christianae, Supplements
Wis.	Wisdom of Solomon
WMANT	Wissenschaftliche Monographien zum Alten und Neuen Testament
WUNT	Wissenschaftliche Untersuchungen zum Neuen Testament
ZNW	*Zeitschrift für die Neutestamentliche Wissenschaft*

Preface

The last decade of the twentieth century has been marked by an explosion of publications on the "Historical Jesus," particularly in the United States. They differ in their assessment of the available sources and of the methods to study them, and therefore give very different pictures of Jesus.

This book does not present a startling new picture of Jesus. In spite of loud claims to the contrary, practically all we are able to know about him comes from the traditions about his actions and sayings recorded in the first three Gospels in the New Testament and from statements of faith in him preserved in Paul's letters. We know Jesus through the responses to him found in these early Christian sources from the first century c.e.

We shall have to work backwards to the earliest responses to Jesus among his followers, and to try to answer the question to what extent these may be traced back to Jesus' own thoughts about his mission. I will argue that we have to assume a basic continuity between the ideas of Jesus' earliest followers and those of Jesus himself. After all, it was Jesus, not someone else, whom the earliest Christians preached.

At the same time, however, it should be clear that we cannot at any point set apart "genuine" words and actions of Jesus not affected by the process of handing down the tradition about him. Our analysis of the material at our disposal is bound to remain tentative, and at all stages of our investigation we have to be very careful. Yet it does seem possible to present what must have been representative of Jesus.

In this study, then, I try to steer a middle course between skepticism and overconfidence with regard to the reliability and the usefulness of what has been handed down. At all stages I have distinguished what seems certain, probable, and possible. We are unable to fill in all the details, yet the result is, I believe, a picture of what was characteristic of Jesus.

This book develops a number of earlier studies on the subject prepared in the past ten years. In particular it links up with my *Jesus, The Servant-Messiah* (1991), a book that grew out of my Shaffer Lectures at Yale Divinity School in February 1989. That book picked up where my *Christology in Context: The Earliest Christian Response to Jesus* (1988) left off.

Jesus, The Servant-Messiah formed the subject of a symposion held at Leiden in January 1991 on the occasion of my retirement as Professor of New Testament and Early Christian Literature. At the symposium my ideas were scrutinized and subjected to constructive criticism by Henk Jan de Jonge, Wayne A. Meeks, and Dieter Lührmann. The lectures held then and the reactions of eight further authors were published in a volume of essays in Dutch that appeared in the same year. The lectures alone are found in English in M. C. de Boer, ed., *From Jesus to John: Essays on Jesus and New Testament Christology in Honour of Marinus de Jonge* (1993). There were also discussions on the Dutch scene about the resurrection of Jesus and about the Parousia, to which Leiden scholars contributed.

So the question of the earliest views on Jesus in relationship to Jesus' own convictions about his mission has kept me busy. Several aspects of the problem were treated in a number of new articles from my hand in the period 1991-1997. After *Jesus, The Servant-Messiah* went out of print, it seemed appropriate to bring together some parts of this earlier study and relevant sections of the new essays, and to weld them together into a new book.

I am grateful for all I learned from the reactions of so many colleagues, not least from talks with Henk Jan de Jonge, my successor in the Leiden chair, and a number of younger scholars in the Leiden Department of New Testament.

Leiden, Easter 1997

CHAPTER 1

Sources and Methods

Anyone who writes about the man Jesus will have to make clear which sources are to be used and what methods are to be applied. As so often the starting point determines the result. Let me briefly outline my position.[1]

Sources

Our principal sources are the Synoptic Gospels. Gospel material that did not make its way into the New Testament, above all that in the *Gospel of Thomas,* has drawn much attention in recent years, but I am not convinced that it offers much help in our quest for Jesus' own views. Among the sayings preserved in the *Gospel of Thomas* and in other sources, there may be early ones of course, but we shall have to prove this in every individual case. Such sayings may corroborate, supplement, or nuance the traditions preserved in the Synoptic Gospels, but they do not allow us to draw a picture of Jesus that is

---

1. See further M. de Jonge, *Christology in Context: The Earliest Christian Response to Jesus* (Philadelphia: Westminster, 1988) 15-30. On sources outside the New Testament, see the careful assessment in J. P. Meier, *A Marginal Jew: Rethinking the Historical Jesus,* vol. 1 (New York: Doubleday, 1991) 112-66. For a survey of recent books on Jesus, see B. Witherington III, *The Jesus Quest: The Third Search for the Jew of Nazareth* (Downers Grove, Ill.: InterVarsity, 1995).

essentially different from that presented in the writings that have become canonical.

With regard to the Synoptics, I take the view that Mark is our oldest Gospel and that Matthew and Luke used not only Mark but also a second source, mainly consisting of sayings of Jesus, commonly designated as Q. We shall have to take into account that the stories and sayings preserved in our sources (not only Mark and Q, but also other possible sources used by Matthew or Luke, and even John) presuppose a stage at which the traditions about Jesus were handed down orally by (groups of) his followers who were convinced that God had raised him from the dead and, for that reason, regarded his words, as well as the reports about his actions, as having continuing importance. What was handed down by mouth and in writing served to evoke and to strengthen faith in the God who had revealed himself decisively in Jesus, and only in a context of faith could those traditions function properly.

I would like to add that we should also pay due attention to the early material in the letters of Paul, the oldest written Christian documents available. Admittedly, very few references to Jesus' earthly life and teaching have survived there — the entire emphasis is on his death and resurrection. In the cultic commemorations of the Last Supper there was a brief reference to the fact that the Lord was handed over to the authorities in the night after his last meal with his disciples (1 Cor. 11:23-26), and in 1 Thess. 2:14-16 the responsibility for the killing of Jesus (and of the prophets before him) is laid upon the Jews. Paul seldom refers to words of Jesus. The few references he does make to them (1 Cor. 7:10, 12, 25; 9:14), even when taken together with a number of allusions, do not offer much to go on. This has often been taken to mean that Paul was interested solely in the fact of Jesus' death and resurrection. But is it plausible that Paul, and the tradition before him, should have spoken about Jesus' death "for us" and used this ancient formula in a hortatory context (Rom. 14:15; 1 Cor. 8:11; 2 Cor. 5:15) without having any further interest in or knowledge of the one who gave his life?

Methods

How can we use the available stories and sayings that were meant to evoke and strengthen faith as sources in our modern historical inquiries?

To me the approach chosen by Nils A. Dahl in his essay "The Problem of the Historical Jesus" (going back to a lecture given in 1952) is still exemplary.[2]

Dahl reminds us that all our evidence has come down to us as recollections about Jesus retained in the tradition of the Christian communities for which the proclamation of the risen Lord was the central element of faith. We should note the word "recollections" here; people wanted to be guided by what Jesus had said and done. Along with many others, Dahl is of the opinion that form criticism "has not yielded objective criteria for separating older from later traditions to the degree expected" (p. 93). Sayings varied in the tradition, and kept varying, because they were handed down as words of the living Lord to his communities in their current circumstances. They were transmitted because they remained relevant.

A clear differentiation between pure history and later theology is impossible. Yet, in Dahl's opinion, "the gospel tradition permits us to draw a very clear picture of what was typical and characteristic of Jesus" (p. 95). He suggests that we examine cross sections of the tradition and analyze sayings and reports of differing form and genre, transmitted in various layers of the tradition. In so doing we will find a number of linking characteristics, such as Jesus' proclamation of the kingdom of God, his position with respect to the law, and his attitude toward various groups in society.

The cross-section method should be supplemented, Dahl suggests, by drawing longitudinal lines leading from Judaism through the figure of Jesus to primitive Christianity. "The historical Jesus is to be found at the crossroad where Christianity and Judaism begin separating from each other, although it has become clear that their paths parted in such a way that Christianity appeared as a new religion alongside Judaism" (p. 95). In other words, we must view Jesus in the context of the Palestinian Judaism of his day and at the same time work backward from the various formulations of primitive Christianity toward the man who is at their center.

2. A Norwegian version was published in 1953, a German one in 1955. The English translation has appeared in various collections of essays but is now most easily accessible in N. A. Dahl, *Jesus the Christ: The Historical Origins of Christological Doctrine* (ed. D. H. Juel; Minneapolis: Fortress, 1991) 81-112; the page numbers given below in parentheses refer to this work. Dahl's lecture was held at a time of renewed interest in the life of Jesus; it was an independent contribution to the so-called New Quest of the Historical Jesus, in which a number of pupils of Rudolf Bultmann played a major role.

Dahl's way out of the impasse created by the nature of our sources is valuable. He does not need to rely on Mark in order to have a framework for arranging individual traditions, nor does he need to assume or to prove the historicity of individual sayings or anecdotes. His cross-section method, called by others the "criterion of multiple attestation," guarantees at least a reasonable degree of certainty about a number of common characteristics. His complementary longitudinal approach allows us to broaden our scope. It enables us both to compare developments in contemporary Judaism and relate them to opinions and attitudes attributed to Jesus, and to examine the notions current in early Christianity and surmise to what extent they originated in what Jesus said and did during his public ministry.

Dahl calls for radical criticism. The authenticity of each individual piece of tradition has to be demonstrated, not the inauthenticity (as some more conservative critics have argued). On the one hand, there is the minimum requirement, which is often called "the criterion of dis-similarity": what can be neither derived from Judaism nor attributed to primitive Christianity can be considered to go back to Jesus. Dahl (with many others) is right in warning us that this is only one heuristic principle among others, though, and yields only the barest minimum. It excludes all that Jesus had in common with his fellow Jews and all that primitive Christianity took over from its master. Dahl, therefore, adds a maximum requirement: "On the other hand, the total tradition concerning Jesus must be taken into consideration. In its totality it is the theology of the church, but at the same time it is also in its totality reflex of Jesus' activity — a *maximum* that contains everything of im-portance for our historical knowledge about Jesus" (p. 97). Our task is to narrow as much as possible the gap between the maximum of the tradition and the critically ensured minimum. It will not be possible to reconstruct a biography of Jesus, and, because our sources are not interested in it, we know nothing of Jesus' inner life. But we can recon-struct a reasonably clear picture of the main lines of Jesus' mission and the essence of his teaching.

We should view the early traditions about Jesus as recollections and response. People looked for guidance from Jesus, whom they believed to be the living Lord. All he had said and done during his public ministry remained of essential value to them. Starting from our earliest written sources, we shall have to work our way backward and try to get as far back as we can — if at all possible, to the time before Jesus' death and to the

4

responses of his followers who heard him preach and saw him act. Wayne A. Meeks has emphasized that we never really know a person apart from the multiple responses to that person on the part of others.[3] We may even say that a person's identity consists in that person's constant interaction with others. This is true and cannot be denied. Yet, that we are able to catch some glimpses of the disciples' responses in the time before their master's death remains of great importance, because these were elicited by the words and actions of the man Jesus, which were intensified as well as clarified in continuous interaction with him. The boundary between "explicit" (i.e., express statements by Jesus about his relationship to God) and "implicit" (i.e., what may be inferred from Jesus' view of his mission with regard to his identity) may be difficult to establish,[4] but we shall have to take these responses of the disciples seriously as reactions to a person who was in a position to respond to them.[5] And if it is difficult to establish that Jesus and his followers agreed in a certain case, it is equally hazardous to claim that, though the disciples held a particular opinion, their master did not agree with them.

The Criteria of Dissimilarity and of Multiple Attestation

Some further remarks on the criteria of dissimilarity and of multiple attestation are in order. Some twenty-five years ago Leander E. Keck warned us in his *A Future for the Historical Jesus* against "the tyranny of the negative criteria."[6] It is right to look for the very words of Jesus (the so-called *ipsissima verba Jesu*), he says, but it is wrong to think that words that can *not* be demonstrated to be authentic may not transmit sound tradition. We are not allowed to obliterate the differences between Jesus and early Christianity, but we should not study our literature as

3. W. A. Meeks, "Asking Back to Jesus' Identity," in M. C. de Boer, ed., *From Jesus to John: Essays on Jesus and New Testament Christology in Honour of Marinus de Jonge* (JSNTSup 84; Sheffield: Sheffield Academic Press, 1993) 38-50, especially 48-50.

4. I return to this below, especially in Chapters 8 and 9.

5. A person's inner self or self-awareness is never adequately communicated to others and therefore can never be the object of historical inquiry — in the case of Jesus or anyone else.

6. L. E. Keck, *A Future for the Historical Jesus: The Place of Jesus in Preaching and Theology* (Nashville: Abingdon, 1971).

if the church "did not consider itself also accountable to Jesus and to its tradition of him" (p. 32). A good example is the summary of Jesus' preaching in Mark 1:14-15. Keck says: "This is almost universally acknowledged to be at the same time a formulation by the church and an accurate summary of what Jesus had to say" (p. 32).

The main negative criterion is that of dissimilarity, which regards as genuine only material that cannot be attributed to the early church on the one side or to Judaism on the other. "Inevitably," says Keck, "the quest for distinctive materials led to a distinctive Jesus" (p. 33), and the result was an incomplete, distorted picture of him. We should not look for the distinctive, but the characteristic Jesus, and this will turn out in all likelihood to be a person capable of holding diverse motives in tension. He will certainly not comply with the standards of consistency applied by modern scholarship. Moreover, given the variety in Judaism around the beginning of the common era and our limited knowledge of it, our failure to find a Jewish parallel for a particular notion attributed to Jesus cannot lead to the conclusion that Jesus is unique in this matter and that the words involved are therefore authentic. In such a case, we can only observe that this particular notion is otherwise unattested.[7]

Also with a view to distinguishing between genuine utterances of Jesus and statements stemming from early Christian believers, the criterion of dissimilarity can only be used with extreme caution because of our lack of knowledge of early Christianity. Form-critical and redaction-critical analysis of literary utterances and the reconstruction of the *Sitz im Leben* and historical situations that form its counterpart are, of necessity, hypothetical to a considerable degree. Moreover, M. Eugene Boring has reminded us that the criterion under discussion may be applied very strictly, limiting the genuine words of Jesus to those which cannot possibly be ascribed to early Christianity, or somewhat more liberally, ascribing to Jesus a great many words that need not necessarily be early Christian.[8] In both cases we remain hampered by our lack of dependable detailed knowledge of christological development in the early Christian communities.

7. This has been rightly pointed out by E. P. Sanders, *Jesus and Judaism* (London: SCM, 1985) 138.

8. M. E. Boring, "The Historical-Critical Method's 'Criteria of Authenticity': The Beatitudes in Q and Thomas as a Test Case," in C. W. Hedrick, ed., *The Historical Jesus and the Rejected Gospels* (*Semeia* 44; Atlanta: Scholars Press, 1988) 9-44; on the criterion of dissimilarity, see 17-21.

We cannot expect much more when we apply the criterion of multiple attestation. This criterion takes seriously that the early Christians wished to relate their convictions to Jesus and acted accordingly when they handed down traditions concerning him. Any tradition process presupposes continuity, and this has to be honored by students of early Christianity who wish to determine what lies at the root of a particular tradition. At the same time, the tradition process is equally characterized by continuous change;[9] one does not transmit matters belonging to the past unless they can be shown to be relevant, or can be made relevant, for the present. Hence, if we try to trace back various lines, starting from Mark, Q, and early traditions in the Pauline letters (of course, more sources may be included, even noncanonical ones, as long as they can be shown not to have branched off later in the tradition process), we may find converging lines enabling us to define a core of early traditions. To prove that this core belongs to the period "before Easter" and that it represents the convictions of Jesus' followers during his lifetime (at least in the last period before his death), or even of Jesus himself, is difficult, and the result is likely to remain to some extent hypothetical, at least as far as individual anecdotes and sayings are concerned. The overall picture that emerges when we view all these individual cases together would, however, seem reliable. Of course, this approach will always have to be combined with other ones.

The Early Christian Kerygma and the Man Jesus

At this point we should stress that it is proper for us to use not only traditions concerning Jesus' actions and sayings during his life, but also

---

9. The element of continuous change is underrated by B. Witherington, III, *The Christology of Jesus* (Minneapolis: Augsburg Fortress, 1990). He presents a remarkably full and detailed picture of Jesus' teaching in various matters. In general, he prefers the criterion of multiple attestation to that of dissimilarity. Of the latter he says: "Only when we find material that can be shown to clearly contradict the core established by the criterion of dissimilarity can a negative verdict be pronounced on a tradition that does not meet the criterion of dissimilarity" (p. 28). This approach, coupled with a readiness to pass judgments on the likelihood of the provenance of certain words in Jesus' own time or in the early church, leads to his overly detailed description of Jesus' christology. See also my review in *SJT* 46 (1993) 264-67.

statements of faith in Jesus that clearly date from the time after his death. Jesus remained central in Christian life and thought, and creedal statements and other utterances of faith are concerned with him. It can be demonstrated in particular that the belief in Jesus' resurrection and the attempts to explain Jesus' death by assigning a positive meaning to that event presuppose the conviction that Jesus was a righteous person completely devoted to God's cause. Next, Christians claimed that Jesus' death and resurrection brought a definitive change in the history of the world. They would never have asserted that if Jesus himself had not announced the coming of the kingdom of God and even seen himself as inaugurating this reign.[10]

Let us look briefly at the early Christian proclamation concerning Jesus' resurrection. Many have maintained that we can speak of a Christian kerygma, and a christology in the proper sense of the word, only *after* the decisive impulse given by the Easter experiences. This has been disputed by Henk Jan de Jonge in a penetrating essay.[11] According to him "the Christian message about Jesus did not originate immediately after his death because of visionary experiences or the discovery of a tomb he had left empty; it is the continuation of the positive response that the historical Jesus evoked in the minds of his disciples already before his death." De Jonge takes as starting point the early Christian formula in 1 Cor. 15:3b-5a and especially the clause "and that he appeared to Cephas." According to him a report about an appearance to

---

10. For what follows, see also M. de Jonge, "Jezus' volstrekte toewijding aan God als kernelement in de vroegste christologie," in A. van de Beek et al., *Waar is God in deze tijd? De betekenis van de geschiedenis in de theologie van Dr. H. Berkhof* (Nijkerk: Callenbach, 1994) 129-42, especially 133-36.

11. H. J. de Jonge, "Visionaire ervaring en de historische oorsprong van het christendom" (Inaugural Lecture, University of Leiden, January 17, 1992). The quotations below are from translations of passages of this lecture. There are a number of further publications from his hand, all in Dutch: "Ontstaan en ontwikkeling van het geloof in Jezus' opstanding," in F. O. van Gennep et al., *Waarlijk opgestaan! Een discussie over de opstanding van Jezus Christus* (2d ed.; Baarn: Ten Have, 1994) 31-50 and "De opstanding van Jezus: De joodse traditie achter een christelijke belijdenis," in T. Baarda et al., eds., *Jodendom en vroeg christendom: Continuïteit en discontinuïteit* (Kampen: Kok, 1991) 47-61. H. J. de Jonge also refers to M. de Jonge, "Jesus' Death for Others and the Death of the Maccabean Martyrs" in idem, *Jewish Eschatology, Early Christian Christology and the Testaments of the Twelve Patriarchs: Collected Essays* (ed. H. J. de Jonge; NovTSup 63; Leiden: Brill, 1991) 125-134. See also M. de Jonge, *Jesus, The Servant-Messiah* (New Haven: Yale University Press, 1991) 56-62.

Peter must have circulated in 35 c.e. at the latest. The term "to appear" serves to denote manifestations of God and of angels. It is important to note that one cannot state that Christ manifested himself in the experience of a human being (Cephas) unless one is first convinced that Christ is a living reality. The stories of Jesus' appearances presuppose his resurrection, just as stories about appearances of God presuppose the reality of God. How could this conviction arise?

Along with other scholars, de Jonge points to the Jewish concept of the suffering righteous person vindicated by God. The righteous one suffers because of his faithful obedience to God and to his will, and he may expect salvation and rehabilitation from God (sometimes these take place through and after death). At the same time one should pay attention to the concept of martyrdom found in 2 Maccabees. Those who are martyred because of their obedience to God's law receive from God a new life after their gruesome death in a renewed, incorruptible, heavenly body (2 Maccabees 7; cf. 15:12-16). One could believe in such an intervention by God "in the case of every righteous person whose faithfulness to God led to the death of a martyr. After Jesus' death at the cross his followers believed this with regard to Jesus. It was simply inherent in their view of Jesus as a righteous person who had to suffer and to die."

If this was the case, Jesus' complete devotion to God's cause must have been an essential element in early Christian belief concerning Jesus. During their many contacts with their master, Jesus' followers must have become convinced that he was a righteous person, completely faithful and obedient to God — even in suffering and death, as turned out later. This faithfulness to God and the circumstances leading to Jesus' death at the cross were the subject of further thought and discussion in the circles of Jesus' followers. Their recollections, in the form of anecdotes about instances in Jesus' life and of sayings uttered by him, were essential aspects of the message about Jesus as the one whom God had raised from the dead and who had appeared to Peter and to other followers.

Jesus' perfect obedience to God was also an essential element in the message concerning Jesus' death. One could, of course, contrast God's activity with the acts of human beings and state: men killed him, but God raised him and gave him glory. This contrasting pattern is found in various speeches of the apostles in the book of Acts.[12] But already at an early stage other explanations of Jesus' death were formu-

12. See de Jonge, *Christology in Context*, 108-9.

lated. In the next chapter I shall describe in some detail three Jewish models of interpretation that were used to explain Jesus' death. Two have already been mentioned by H. J. de Jonge: the concept of the suffering righteous one, and the notion of the martyr who is faithful to the law of God. The third is that of the prophet of God who is rejected and killed by Israel and/or its leaders.

We may now take one further step. Characteristic of early Christian views about Jesus is the conviction that Jesus was not just a prophet, but the last and *final* envoy of the God of Israel, and that he was a righteous person and a martyr whose death and vindication brought a decisive and *definitive* turn in the history of humanity. To put it differently: with him the time of the end had already begun. Jesus was an eschatological figure who had inaugurated the new era in God's dealings with Israel and the world. This notion is not inherent in the notion of the resurrection of a martyr,[13] neither is it connected with any of the Jewish models of interpretation used to explain Jesus' suffering and death. Our conclusion has to be that already before Jesus' death his followers must have believed that he was the herald and inaugurator of God's reign. If that is so, it is important to examine Jesus' words concerning the kingdom of God.[14]

Outline of the Present Study

After our findings above, the next few steps are evident. In Chapter 2 we will look more closely at the models used to interpret Jesus' death. This will be followed by an examination of Jesus' sayings concerning

13. We should distinguish between resurrection, the rehabilitation of an individual after death, and the collective resurrection at the end of time. Both were, of course, connected in early Christianity, for instance by Paul in 1 Corinthians 15. See the publications by H. J. de Jonge mentioned above in note 11, and J. Holleman, *Resurrection and Parousia: A Traditio-Historical Study of Paul's Eschatology in 1 Corinthians 15* (NovT-Sup 84; Leiden: Brill, 1996).

14. The eschatological element in Jesus' preaching must not be overlooked; explaining it away leads to fundamental misunderstanding. See B. Chilton, *Pure Kingdom: Jesus' Vision of God* (Grand Rapids: Eerdmans, 1996). With regard to the kingdom of God, see J. P. Meier, *A Marginal Jew: Rethinking the Historical Jesus,* vol. 2 (New York: Doubleday, 1994) 237-508.

the kingdom of God in Mark and Q, as well as of some Pauline texts on the subject, in Chapter 3.

Chapter 3 ends with a few observations and questions. First, characteristic of Jesus' view of the kingdom of God is his insistence on its (speedy) future manifestation as well as on its dynamic presence in his own words and actions. Is this typical only of Jesus (and, similarly, of early Christian eschatology), or are there parallels in contemporary writings? This question, together with some other ones, is addressed in Chapter 4.

Next, there is the question how Jesus' preaching about the kingdom of God was related to his views of his suffering, death, and vindication by God. The solution of this problem requires no less than three chapters. Chapter 5 looks again at the sayings about the future manifestation of God's kingdom (particularly Mark 14:25) and arrives at the conclusion that these texts do not mention a central role for Jesus; all emphasis is on the final realization of *God's* sovereign rule.

Chapter 6 discusses the many texts about the future which assign a central position to *Jesus'* coming.

Chapter 7 tries to explain the seeming discrepancy between the results of Chapters 5 and 6 by examining the texts about Jesus as Son of Man, particularly (again) those dealing with the future. It puts forward the hypothesis that Jesus may have envisaged his vindication as messenger of God's kingdom as an *exaltation* to ruler and judge at the moment of God's definitive intervention. Later this led to the conception of his *coming* to earth in this capacity.

Chapter 8 takes up a third problem formulated at the end of Chapter 3. Jesus' role in the inauguration of God's rule on earth implies a christology. To what extent did this lead to an explicit use of "christological" designations on his part? Chapter 8 thus deals with the topic "Jesus as Messiah and Son of God."

Chapter 9 speaks about the relationship between christology and theology in the context of Jesus' and early Christian expectations about God's intervention in the future. Here I do not limit myself to the earliest responses to Jesus anymore, but ask also how this theme was treated at later stages of christological thinking, including that represented by the Gospel of John. Chapter 10 deals with the same subject from a different angle: How could early Christians reconcile their christologies, centering on Jesus and making considerable claims for him, with the worship of the One God of Israel? Both chapters emphasize the "theocentricity" of all christology.

CHAPTER 2

Jesus' Mission and Death on the Cross

Jesus' life ended on the cross, a fact of crucial importance for early and present-day Christians alike. The value and significance of the crucifixion are inextricably bound up with Jesus' person, with his intentions and his own understanding of his death as the consummation of his mission. In itself the crucifixion was merely a wanton (if legal) execution of one out of many — an event, for that matter, hardly likely to be recorded in history. It would have been a fate suffered by one individual, devoid of greater implications. For his followers it was essential to explain why this happened to their master. If they had not been convinced that Jesus actively participated in the events leading up to a death that he accepted of his own free will in obedience to God, this death could never have become the supreme sacrifice that it is within Christianity's scheme of reference. Following the inner logic of Jesus' entire mission, it formed its apogee in the purest sense of the word.

For that reason I shall attempt to determine what can be known about Jesus' own attitude toward his death. Did he foresee it? Did he even seek it out? What meaning did he attach to it in view of the mission entrusted to him by God?

In line with the arguments developed earlier, I shall take as my starting point the various interpretations of Jesus' death found in the oldest strata of traditional Christian material. Only then shall I take into account a number of sayings of Jesus recorded in the Synoptic Gospels and try to determine to what extent they convey or reflect what Jesus thought and said and how they fit into the context of what is reported about his actions.[1]

The traditional expressions and patterns of though stem from the communities of the earliest followers of Jesus after his death. This death, a shattering event, had to be explained. Its meaning had to be understood both in the context of Jesus' own mission and in view of their conviction that this mission was now being continued, thanks to Jesus' victory over death. Jesus' followers believed in a living Lord who guided their lives through the Spirit and who would return in order to realize the sovereign rule of God on earth, which he had announced and inaugurated during his mission in Galilee and Judea.

In their attempts to grasp the meaning of Jesus' death, his followers were led by their conviction that Jesus had indeed been sent by God at a crucial moment in history and that God had vindicated him. He had died on the cross, but he was no criminal or revolutionary, much less a pious man or a prophet who, in the eyes of his executioners, had deluded his followers and himself. Not only was the message of Jesus' death on the cross, in the words of Paul, a "stumbling block to Jews and folly to Gentiles" (1 Cor. 1:23), an impediment to hostile opponents and interested outsiders alike; also for those who firmly believed in the continuing leadership of their living master, his death required clarification. Meditating on the divine "necessity" of Jesus' death (Mark 8:31) and combing the scriptures (see, for instance, 1 Cor. 15:3-4, with the phrase "in accordance with the scriptures" and Mark 14:21), they searched for other examples of servants of God who had suffered and died and had been vindicated. What had been taught about them was used to explain what had happened to Jesus.

From the very beginning, various models of interpretation were applied, and as Christian reflection continued, the variety became even

---

1. A crucial sifting of the synoptic material is found in the thorough and stimulating collection of essays by Heinz Schürmann, *Jesu ureigener Tod: Exegetische Besinnungen und Ausblick* (Freiburg: Herder, 1975); idem, *Gottes Reich — Jesu Geschick: Jesu ureigener Tod im Licht seiner Basileia-Verkündigung* (Freiburg: Herder, 1983). See also P. Pokorny, *The Genesis of Christology: Foundations for a Theology of the New Testament* (Edinburgh: Clark, 1987), translation of *Die Entstehung der Christologie* (Berlin: Evangelische Verlagsanstalt, 1985), who discusses Jesus of Nazareth (pp. 14-62) before dealing with the oldest testimonies of faith in the long section that bears the title "The Decisive Impulse," 63-167.

greater. For our purposes I shall concentrate on three conceptions found in traditional material incorporated in Paul, Q, and Mark: (a) the interpretation of Jesus' death as that of an envoy of God rejected by Israel; (b) the conception of Jesus as a suffering, righteous servant of God; and (c) the view of Jesus' death as a death for others.[2]

These models of interpretation are not mutually exclusive but complementary, if only because they aim at elucidating essential aspects of the life and death (and continuing activity) of one person, Jesus. We shall find, however, that these approaches cannot, either individually or taken together, explain everything about Jesus. Jesus is not just any messenger sent by God, but the ultimate envoy; he is not just any suffering, righteous servant of God, but servant and Son of God par excellence. In one type of formula for speaking about Jesus' death for others, we find *Christos* as subject: "*Christ* died for us (you)." The use of this designation for Jesus is one indication that with his death (and resurrection) a definitive turning point has been reached, a new era has begun. Along with all the discontinuity, which should be neither denied nor belittled, there is also continuity between the Christian kerygma after Easter and Jesus' announcement and inauguration of God's kingdom before Easter, which includes the call for a decision concerning his own person.

Our task is to determine in what respects the interpretations given after Easter presuppose the views of Jesus' life and death held by his followers even before his death on the cross. In doing so, cautious but persistent "asking back" may perhaps lead us to aspects of Jesus' *own* interpretation of his life and death in faithful obedience to God — however difficult (or even, in the end, impossible) it may be to reconstruct the precise words spoken by Jesus and to determine his exact actions.

---

2. See also M. de Jonge, *Christology in Context: The Earliest Christian Response to Jesus* (Philadelphia: Westminster, 1988) 173-88, 208-11; idem, "Jesus' Death for Others and the Death of the Maccabean Martyrs," in T. Baarda et al., eds., *Text and Testimony: Essays in Honour of A. F. J. Klijn* (Kampen: Kok, 1988) 142-51, now in idem, *Jewish Eschatology, Early Christian Christology, and the Testaments of the Twelve Patriarchs: Collected Essays* (NovTSup 63; Leiden: Brill, 1991) 125-34. A very good survey of the available material is given in M. L. Gubler, *Die frühesten Deutungen des Todes Jesu: Eine motivgeschichtliche Darstellung aufgrund der neueren exegetischen Forschung* (OBO 15; Freiburg: Universitätsverlag; Göttingen: Vandenhoeck & Ruprecht, 1977).

Jesus as an Envoy of God Rejected by Israel

In Paul's first letter to the Thessalonians we find a bitter reproach by the Jew Paul of those Jews who "killed both the Lord Jesus and the prophets, and drove us out, and displease God and oppose all men by hindering us from speaking to the Gentiles that they may be saved — so as always to fill up the measure of their sins. But God's wrath has come upon them for ever" (2:15-16, RSV margin). In this passage, a small digression in the letter, Paul draws on traditional material to link the killing of Jesus, who is named first and is expressly called "the Lord," with the killing of the prophets and the persecution of Jesus' followers.[3] He emphasizes that the iniquity of the Jews is now complete. The limit has been reached; the hour of judgment has arrived.

A similar view is found in the Q passage Luke 11:49-51 (par. Matt. 23:34-36). In Luke's version, very likely representing that of Q, we read: "Therefore also the Wisdom of God said, 'I will send them prophets and apostles, some of whom they will kill and persecute,' that the blood of all the prophets, shed from the foundation of the world, may be required of this generation. . . . Yes I tell you, it shall be required of this generation." Again it is stressed that the climax has been reached, that judgment and punishment are at hand. Among the prophets and envoys sent by Wisdom are John the Baptist and Jesus, who in the Q passage Luke 7:31-35 (par. Matt. 11:16-19) are called "the children of Wisdom" — both rejected by "this generation," though for different reasons. Of course, Christian messengers after Jesus are also included. Matthew, who has Jesus himself announce the persecution, mentions only prophets and wise men sent by Jesus. The announcement is found in Luke and

---

3. Because Paul is following a traditional line of argument for a moment, he says more than is strictly necessary in this context. It is noteworthy that he starts by speaking about the Jews in Judea but finally includes all Jews who oppose his preaching to the Gentiles. He adds, "oppose all men," a standard feature of pagan anti-Jewish sentiment. I see no reason to regard these verses, or part of them, as later interpolation. See the well documented article by T. Baarda, "Maar de toorn is over hen gekomen (I Thess. 2:16c)," in T. Baarda et al., *Paulus en de andere Joden: Exegetische bijdragen en discussie* (Delft: Meinema, 1984) 15-74. On this difficult and controversial passage, see also I. Broer, "'Der ganze Zorn ist schon über sie gekommen': Bemerkungen zur Interpretationshypothese und zur Interpretation von 1 Thess 2, 14-16," in R. F. Collins, ed., *The Thessalonian Correspondence* (BETL 87; Leuven: Leuven University Press and Peeters, 1990) 137-59; cf. also, in the same volume, T. Holtz, "The Judgment on the Jews and the Salvation of All Israel: 1 Thess 2, 15-16 and Rom 11, 25-26" (pp. 284-94).

in Matthew in the context of a whole series of accusations against the Pharisees and the scribes or lawyers. Matthew adds the well-known saying, "O Jerusalem, Jerusalem, killing the prophets and stoning those who are sent to you!" (23:37, identical with Luke 13:34, though placed in a different context there). Mark offers the parable of the vineyard, in which the son of the vineyard's owner is killed as his father's final envoy after a number of messengers have been beaten, wounded, and killed (Mark 12:1-9). The son stands for Jesus, the other messengers for the prophets. Again, God's intervention is said to be at hand. The owner of the vineyard "will come and destroy the tenants, and give the vineyard to others" (v. 9).

This theme, then, is found in Pauline material, in Q, and in Mark. We may add Luke 6:22-23 (par. Matt. 5:11-12) — a Q passage in which the persecution of Jesus' followers is compared to that of the prophets earlier in history — and Acts 7:51-53, where Stephen, about to be martyred himself, accuses the Jews of persecuting and betraying and murdering him whose coming they announced. As Odil H. Steck has shown in a very detailed study, the early Christian statements fit into a series of passages found in the Old Testament and other ancient Jewish writings that criticize Israel's rejection of the prophets who are sent again and again to bring Israel back to a life of obedience to God.[4]

This line of interpretation was clearly popular among early Christians: it explained not only the death of Jesus but also the sufferings and persecutions they themselves were subjected to by the Jewish authorities. Israel had acted like this all the time! Only *now* the measure of sins was full; with the killing of God's final envoy, Jesus, the decisive turning point had come.

Interestingly, this model of interpretation (which emphasizes the negative response of the persecutors rather than the obedience and faithfulness of the messengers) does not speak of Jesus' resurrection as his vindication. After the parable in 12:1-9, to be sure, Mark adds a reference to the resurrection by quoting Ps. 118:22-23, and Acts 7:51-53 is followed in verse 55 by a vision of Jesus standing at the right hand

4. O. H. Steck, *Israel und das gewaltsame Geschick der Propheten: Untersuchungen zur Überlieferung des deuteronomistischen Geschichtsbildes im Alten Testament, Spätjudentum, und Urchristentum* (WMANT 23; Neukirchen-Vluyn: Neukirchener Verlag, 1967).

of God in heaven.[5] But the basic pattern implies the vindication of Jesus, his followers, and all preceding messengers at the impending judgment on Israel. Strikingly, no positive meaning is attached to Jesus' death or to that of others.

Those who handed down words of Jesus like the ones from Q and Mark just cited did so because of the connection and continuity they saw between themselves and the disciples who had followed Jesus during his lifetime and had been sent out on incidental missions by Jesus himself. Then and now, solidarity between pupil and master, envoy and sender, counted.

We are not in a position to determine exactly the authentic kernel in the words on discipleship found in Mark and Q. But if we compare, for example, Mark 8:34–9:1 (par.) and 10:17-31 (par.)[6] with Luke 14:26-27 (par. Matt. 10:37-38) and Luke 9:57-62 (par. Matt. 8:18-22), or if we read Mark's account of the commissioning of the Twelve in 6:6b-13 beside the corresponding Q pericope in Luke 10:2-12 (par. Matt. 9:37-38; 10:16, 9-13, 7-8a, 14-15), we find many converging statements.

Preaching and healing in the name of their master, the disciples will meet with the opposition and rejection he himself had to face. Mark places the commissioning of the Twelve appositely after the story of Jesus' rejection at Nazareth as an illustration of the truth of the proverb "a prophet is not without honor, except in his own country and among his own kin, and in his own house" (Mark 6:4). It is followed by the story of the killing of John the Baptist by Herod Antipas (6:17-29).

Q has preserved the condemnation of the Galilean cities of Chorazin, Bethsaida, and Capernaum (Luke 10:13-15, par. Matt. 11:20-24). In the final judgment it will be more tolerable for Tyre and Sidon than for the inhabitants of these three cities, because they did not repent after the mighty works done in them — by Jesus himself, according to Luke, who connects this passage with that of the commissioning of the Seventy. Another Q passage, Luke 11:29-32 (par. Matt. 12:38-42), compares the reaction of the present evil generation unfavorably with the

---

5. The contrast pattern employed in the speeches in Acts (e.g., Acts 2:23-24: "This Jesus . . . you crucified and killed by the hand of lawless men. But God raised him up") also emphasizes the responsibility of the Jewish leaders for Jesus' death. It adds a resurrection formula stressing God's initiative in raising Jesus from the dead. For details see my *Christology in Context*, 108-11.

6. Cf. also Mark 10:35-45 and par.

response of Nineveh to Jonah and of the Queen of the South to Solomon. The Ninevites "repented at the preaching of Jonah, and behold, something greater than Jonah is here" (v. 32) just as "something greater than Solomon is here" (v. 31).

Jesus was met with unbelief and rejection, as were his disciples. John the Baptist, another messenger of God who came immediately before Jesus and was directly linked with him, had been murdered. It is extremely likely that not only Jesus' followers but also Jesus himself viewed John's fate, the opposition they faced, and the possibility of violent death for themselves, in the light of those passages from scripture that denounced Israel's violent rejection of messengers sent by God.

Jesus as a Suffering Righteous Servant

In Luke 6:22-23 (par. Matt. 5:11-12) the exclusion and reviling of Jesus' followers on account of the Son of Man ("on my account," Matt. 5:11) is compared with the persecution of the prophets by their (the Jews') fathers. Yet this suffering is also a reason for joy: "Your reward is great in heaven." Those who suffer hardship because of Jesus are blessed, just as those who are poor shall receive the kingdom of God, those who hunger now shall be satisfied, and those who weep now shall laugh (Luke 6:20-21, par. Matt. 5:3, 6, [4]). The series of four beatitudes found in Luke very likely marked the beginning of Jesus' teaching in Q. When the kingdom of God, now breaking forth on earth, becomes full reality, then poverty, hunger, and sorrow will vanish and those who remain faithful to the one who has inaugurated this kingdom will be rewarded by God. Mark 13:9-13 (and par.), depicting the troubles that lie ahead for those who wish to remain loyal to the message of the Gospel, ends with the assurance, "But he who endures to the end will be saved" (see also Matt. 10:22). Similarly, in the section on the consequences of discipleship in Mark 8:34–9:1 (and par.) we find the promise that "whoever loses his life for my sake and the gospel's will save it" (v. 35, par. Matt. 16:25; Luke 9:24; John 12:25 and Matt. 10:39, par. Luke 17:33 [Q]). That person will have a share in the kingdom of God when it reveals itself in power inaugurated by the Son of Man coming "in the glory of his Father with the holy angels" (8:38; 9:1 and par.).

According to these words of Jesus found in Mark and Q, those who follow Jesus, bringing his message and serving his cause until the very end, will be vindicated. They may expect to suffer and must be ready to give their lives, but they may also expect to share in the blessings of God's kingdom, due to be revealed in the near future.

Mark connects the announcement of the sufferings and vindication of the disciples with the first of three predictions of Jesus' passion and resurrection "after three days" that figure prominently in his Gospel (8:31; 9:31; 10:33-34). After all, Jesus' disciples are called upon to *become his followers.* However, the first and, even more so, the third of these predictions have been modeled on the events recorded later in this Gospel and refer to Jesus' resurrection immediately after his death (without mentioning the arrival of God's kingdom). The short prediction in 9:31 — "The Son of man will be delivered into the hands of men, and they will kill him; and when he is killed, after three days he will rise" — has been thought to go back to Jesus himself. As C. K. Barrett has said: "If . . . Jesus did (in forms not fully recoverable) predict and interpret his approaching passion, the interpretation must have included the prediction of some kind of vindication beyond the passion. It is inconceivable that Jesus simply predicted the complete and final failure of his mission."[7] He regards it as possible that the words "after three days he will rise," which in their *present* context point forward to Mark 16:1-8 (cf. the ancient formula from 1 Cor. 15:3-5, with the phrase "he was raised on the third day"), originally indicated Jesus' exaltation and vindication a short time after his violent death. Barrett has drawn attention to Mark 14:25: "Truly, I say to you, I shall not drink again the fruit of the vine until that day when I drink it new in the kingdom of God" (cf. Luke 22:15-18). These words, spoken at the last meal that Jesus shares with his disciples, look beyond the imminent passion to Jesus' participation in the joys of the fully realized kingdom. We shall have to return to this later.[8]

In support of the thesis that Jesus himself may have been convinced that his passion would be followed by his vindication (in whatever form), we may point to the rich and variegated tradition found in the Old Testament and other early Jewish literature of God's rescuing his faithful servants who, though in distress, poverty, or oppression,

7. C. K. Barrett, *Jesus and the Gospel Tradition* (London: SPCK, 1967) 76. This book gives the text of the Shaffer Lectures for 1965.

8. See further below, pp. 59-69.

continue to place their trust in him. Jesus is portrayed as a faithful servant of God, living in close communion with God, whom, according to Q, he addressed as Father (see Luke 10:21-22, par. Matt. 11:25-27; 11:2, par. Matt. 6:9; Mark 14:36 and par.; further substantiated by Gal. 4:6 and Rom. 8:15). Jesus is shown as placing his trust in God's power to deliver him and all the faithful.

The theme of God's righteous suffering servant recurs in numerous passages and with many variations in form and content.[9] The vital connection between these servants' complete trust in God and his deliverance of them, reiterated throughout these passages, is expressed in Ps. 34:17-19 with the words:

> When the righteous cry for help, the LORD hears,
> and delivers them out of their troubles.
> The LORD is near to the brokenhearted,
> and saves the crushed in spirit.
> Many are the afflictions of the righteous;
> but the LORD delivers him out of them all.

God often helps the afflicted by bringing a radical turn in their lives — as, for example, in a number of the Psalms (which, consequently, combine lament and prayer with thanksgiving) and in the stories of the three young men in the fiery furnace in Daniel 3 and of Daniel himself in the lions' den in Daniel 6. In Daniel 3 and 6, God's faithful servants are prepared to give their lives for God's sake, but at the crucial moment an angel sent by God comes to their rescue. God faithfully delivered his servants "who trusted in him . . . and yielded up their bodies rather than serve and worship any god except their own God" (Dan. 3:28; cf. 6:20-22, 25-27).

Some texts, many of them apocalyptic ones, go a decisive step further by connecting God's vindication of his faithful servants with his

9. See my *Christology in Context*, 175-79, and the interesting studies of L. Ruppert, *Der leidende Gerechte: Eine motivgeschichtliche Untersuchung zum Alten Testament und zwischentestamentlichen Judentum* (Forschung zur Bibel 5; Würzburg: Echter, 1973); idem, *Jesus als der leidende Gerechte? Der Weg Jesu im Lichte eines alt- und zwischentestamentlichen Motivs* (SBS 59; Stuttgart: Katholisches Bibelwerk, 1972); and K. Th. Kleinknecht, *Der leidende Gerechtfertigte: Die alttestamentlich-jüdische Tradition vom 'leidenden Gerechten' und ihre Rezeption bei Paulus* (WUNT 2/13; Tübingen: Mohr Siebeck, 1984).

final intervention in the affairs of the world, and by introducing the idea of resurrection. This is the case in Dan. 11:29-35 and 12:1-3; *1 Enoch* 102–104; *2 Apoc. Bar.* 48:48-50 and 52:6-7, and in the texts from Q and Mark mentioned above. Special mention should be made of two passages from the Wisdom of Solomon, 2:12-20 and 5:1-7. In the first of these two passages, a righteous man who professes to have knowledge of God, calls himself "servant of God," and knows that God is his father (vv. 13, 16) is condemned to death by his opponents. "Let us see if his words are true, and let us test what will happen at the end of his life, for if the righteous man is God's son, he will help him" (vv. 17-18). God does help him; in 5:1-7 it is his opponents who stand condemned. They have no choice but to confess that he has truly served God. He is "numbered among the sons of God," and "his lot is among the saints" (v. 5). The wicked are dispersed like chaff or smoke before the wind, but the righteous live forever (vv. 14-16). Although, as George Nickelsburg has argued, "the eschatological timetable of Wisdom is far from clear,"[10] these passages seem to suggest that the righteous who are persecuted will be exalted and vindicated without delay, and that their persecutors will have to witness their glory and acknowledge their own guilt after their victims' death before they themselves are destroyed altogether. Whatever the exact timetable, the important point is that God is righteous and faithful to those who obey him completely and place their trust in him.

In the Markan passion story, the words "My God, my God, why hast thou forsaken me" from Psalm 22, one of the psalms of the suffering righteous, are Jesus' last understandable utterance before his death (Mark 15:34; Matt. 27:46). These words are even given in Aramaic before being translated into Greek. Scholars have collected other references, both explicit and implicit, to passages representing the various aspects of the tradition of the suffering righteous, and it is quite possible that even at an earlier stage they helped mold the story of Jesus' passion on the cross.[11] The use of Ps. 22:1 is intended to suggest the expectation

10. George W. E. Nickelsburg, Jr., *Resurrection, Immortality, and Eternal Life in Intertestamental Judaism* (HTS 26; Cambridge: Harvard University Press; London: Oxford University Press, 1972) 88; see the entire section on the Book of Wisdom and related texts on pp. 48-92.

11. George W. E. Nickelsburg, "The Genre and Function of the Markan Passion Narrative," *HTR* 73 (1980) 153-84, has tried to demonstrate in detail that the pre-Markan passion narrative "recounted the death and exaltation of Jesus, employing the

of divine deliverance, I think. Luke, clearly wanting to avoid misunderstanding, replaced the quotation from Ps. 22:1 with a phrase taken from
another psalm of suffering and deliverance, "Into thy hands I commit
my spirit" (Ps. 31:5). Later on in the story, God's vindication of his
suffering servant Jesus is expressed in terms of resurrection and exaltation. In Mark 16:6 the young man in a white robe sitting inside the
empty tomb announces to the women that the crucified Jesus has been
raised; his disciples will see him in Galilee. And at the trial before the
Sanhedrin, just before his condemnation by Pilate and his crucifixion,
Jesus openly declares that he is "the Christ, the Son of the Blessed" and
that those who are about to condemn him "will see the Son of Man
sitting at the right hand of Power, and coming with the clouds of heaven"
(14:61-62).

This scene is reminiscent of that pictured in Wisd. 2:12-20 and
5:1-7, as is the scene of mockery in 15:29-32. The connection is brought
out even more clearly in the parallel passage in Matt. 27:39-43, which
has the additional words, "He trusts in God; let God deliver him now,
if he desires him; for he said 'I am the Son of God.'" In Mark 15:39 the
Roman centurion at the cross declares: "Truly this man was a son of
God!"

For Mark (and the other evangelists) Jesus is not just any servant,
any son of God; he is "the Christ, *the* Son of the Blessed" (14:61). Jesus'
solemn declaration, "I am; and you will see the Son of Man sitting at
the right hand of Power, and coming with the clouds of heaven" (v. 62),
marks a significant turning point in Mark's story. Here Jesus says openly
to his opponents (and indirectly to the readers of this Gospel) who he
is. As George Nickelsburg has said, the use of the genre of the story of
the righteous one in the passion narrative served "to describe how the
death and exaltation of Jesus brought the old order to an end" (p. 183).
It is clear that the convictions and beliefs of the early Christians in the
period after Jesus' death have exercised a considerable influence on the
transmission of the stories brought together in Mark 14–16. We cannot

---

genre of the story of the righteous one" (p. 183). R. Pesch, *Das Markusevangelium*, vol.
2 (HTKNT 2/2; Freiburg: Herder, 1977) 1-27, has given two pages of possible allusions
and references in the pre-Markan history of the passion (to which he assigns much of
8:27–16:8). His conclusion is that "zwei Drittel des Materials der vormk. Passions-
geschichte ist durch Anspielungen bzw. Zitationen von *passio-iusti*-Motiven ausgeprägt"
(p. 13). This is no doubt exaggerated.

base a reconstruction of what factually happened, and of what histori-cally motivated Jesus and his closest followers, on this narrative.

If we wish to maintain that Jesus, in all likelihood, expected not only to suffer and to die but also to be vindicated by God, we must nonetheless be cautious about using the argument that he must have been acquainted with the tradition of God's help for his suffering ser-vants (in its many forms). We should note, however, that his announce-ment of the coming of God's sovereign rule on earth implied the ex-pectation that it would soon be completely realized, and that this, in turn, would bring the vindication of the one who inaugurated it *and* of those who had been sent out by him to preach, exorcise, and heal in his name. Jesus' frequent use of the term "Son of Man," in Mark as well as in Q, may also point in that direction. After all, in Daniel 7 the "one like a son of man" who stands for the saints of the Most High, oppressed by "the little horn" of the fourth beast (vv. 21, 25), receives an everlasting kingdom.[12]

Jesus as the Man Who Died for Others

The notion that Jesus died for others — or, more specifically, for the sins of others — is widespread in the oldest stratum of tradition. The longer expression gives an explanation of the shorter one, as Paul makes clear in Rom. 5:1-11, where he emphasizes that "while we were yet helpless, at the right time Christ died for the ungodly" (v. 6) and "while we were yet sinners Christ died for us" (v. 8). These two statements elaborate on the formula "Christ died for us/you" *(Christos apethanen hyper hēmōn/hymōn)* found in Rom. 14:15; 1 Cor. 8:11 (with the prep-osition *dia* instead of *hyper*); 1 Cor. 15:3 ("for our sins," in the context of a formula dealing with death and resurrection); and 1 Thess. 5:10.[13]

---

12. See further Chapter 7 below.

13. Here, the 26th and 27th editions of Nestle-Aland have *hyper,* whereas the 25th edition preferred *peri* with the original text of Sinaiticus, Vaticanus, and minuscule 33 (with no change of meaning). The authenticity of *peri* in 1 Thess. 5:10 and 1 Cor. 1:13 is defended by H. J. de Jonge, "The Original Setting of the *Christos apethanen huper* Formula," in Collins, ed., *The Thessalonian Correspondence,* 229-35. Compare also 1 Pet. 2:21, "Christ suffered for you," and 3:18, "Christ . . . suffered for sins once and for all." "Suffered" *(epathen)* is very similar to "died" *(apethanen)*. In fact, in 1 Pet. 3:18 Nestle-

23

It is implied as well in Rom. 14:9; 1 Cor. 1:13; 2 Cor. 5:21; and Gal. 2:21; 3:13.[14]

The meaning of the formula is brought out clearly, again by Paul, in 2 Cor. 5:14-15: "For the love of Christ controls us, because we are convinced that one has died for all; therefore all have died. And he died for all, that those who live might live no longer for themselves, but for him who for their sake died and was raised." What happened to the "one" happened to the "many." If, then, Christ died for the sake of those connected with him in faith, they too have died and are under the obligation to live a new life for him who was raised to a new life after his death.

In Rom. 6:2-11 and Gal. 3:26-29 this central idea of a close communion between Jesus Christ and those belonging to him is expressed in connection with baptism. In Galatians 3 all believers are said to be children of God "in Christ Jesus"; in being baptized into Christ they have "put on Christ." In Romans 6 this idea of communion is linked with that of Jesus' death and resurrection. Those who "have been baptized into Christ Jesus were baptized into his death" (v. 3). Paul continues: "We were buried therefore with him by baptism into death, so that as Christ was raised from the dead by the glory of the Father, we too might walk in the newness of life" (v. 4). This form of corporate thinking constitutes an essential element in Paul's theology and may also have been related to corporate experiences in the context of the baptismal ritual.[15]

The *hyper* formulas and the corporate terminology make it clear that what happens to someone who represents others has a direct impact on those associated with that person. In the case of Jesus Christ, if people have sinned and their relationship with God has been disturbed, then the death of one who has not sinned (as Paul states explicitly in 2 Cor. 5:21) effectively restores this relationship and takes away the consequences of sin — for those who put their trust in him and live in communion with him.

Aland, 25th ed., preferred the latter word, which also occurs as a variant in 1 Pet. 2:21 in a considerable number of witnesses. See also Phil. 1:29, where the expression "to suffer for Christ's sake" is used.

14. See also John 11:50, 51; 18:14.

15. See de Jonge, *Christology in Context*, 42, with reference to W. A. Meeks, *The First Urban Christians: The Social World of the Apostle Paul* (New Haven: Yale University Press, 1983) 150-57.

In the traditions surrounding the Last Supper, the same thought is expressed with the help of covenant terminology. The two oldest versions of that story, those found in Mark 14:22-25 and in 1 Cor. 11:23-26 (clearly handed down in a form to be recited at the commemoration of the Lord's death by Christian communities), are worded somewhat differently from each other, but they express the same basic idea. Mark 14:24 speaks of "my blood of the covenant, which is poured out for many" (Matt. 26:28 adds "for the forgiveness of sins"). The word "many" used here (and in Mark 10:45), in the context of the Gospel of Mark suggests the spreading of the gospel message to all nations; in itself it only presupposes the notion of representation also found in 2 Cor. 5:14-15. Paul has "for you" and connects this expression with the bread: "This is my body which is broken for you" (1 Cor 11:24). In the next verse he speaks of "this cup" as the "new covenant in my blood."

To complement this picture we should look briefly at the so-called surrender formulas in which the verbs *paradidonai* ("to give up") and *didonai* ("to give") occur. In the opening of his letter to the Galatians, Paul speaks about "our Lord Jesus Christ who gave himself for our sins" (vv. 3-4); later in the same letter he professes to live by faith in the Son of God, "who loved me and gave himself for me" (2:20). In Rom. 8:32 the agent behind Jesus' sacrifice is God ("He who did not spare his own Son but gave him up for us all"),[16] and in Rom. 4:24-25 he is the implied subject: "Jesus our Lord . . . was put to death for our trespasses and raised for our justification." Additions to the formula try to make clearer what it wants to convey. Eph. 5:2 (cf. v. 25) says: "Christ loved us and gave himself up for us, a fragrant offering and a sacrifice to God," and in Mark 10:45 we encounter the well-known saying "the Son of Man . . . came not to be served but to serve, and to give his life as a ransom for *(anti)* many" (cf. Matt. 20:28; 1 Tim. 2:6; Tit. 2:14).

Wherever the concept of Jesus' death for others is found, it is spoken of as having brought a definitive change in the relationship between God and those who belong to Jesus. It is not just one particular man called Jesus who died; in one way or another, his special status is always emphasized. In the "died for us/you" formulas the subject is usually Christ, and the connection between death and resurrection is

---

16. In "Jesus' Death for Others," 146-47, I have argued that there is no reason to connect this verse with Jewish traditions concerning the "Binding of Isaac" based on Gen. 22:1-19; see also de Jonge, *Christology in Context,* 241, n. 36.

sometimes made explicit. In the surrender formulas the subject is frequently "Son of God" or "Son of Man." Jesus' death has a lasting effect. In Rom. 5:1-11, for instance, Paul links reconciliation with God now to salvation from God's eschatological judgment in the future. In Gal. 1:4 he declares that Jesus Christ "gave himself for our sins to deliver us from the present evil age." Communion is celebrated in expectation of the coming of the kingdom of God. Paul writes, "as you eat this bread and drink the cup, you proclaim the Lord's death until he comes" (1 Cor. 11:26), and, as mentioned previously, Mark includes in his recounting of the Last Supper Jesus' words about drinking the fruit of the vine new in the kingdom of God (14:25). In short, this interpretation of Jesus' death as the supreme sacrifice on behalf of humankind, to be accepted in faith, is firmly embedded in the Christian view of Jesus' mission as the decisive turning point in God's dealings with Israel and the world. It is clear that in this pattern of thought Jesus' death cannot be regarded separately from his life. His death could not have served God's purpose had his life not been dedicated to the service of God and humankind all along. When Paul writes, "For our sake he made him to be sin who knew no sin" (2 Cor. 5:21), he expresses what was common conviction. The one who gave his life as a ransom for many came not to be served but to serve (Mark 10:45). The Lukan parallel to this saying, given in the context of Jesus' last meal with his disciples (Luke 22:25-27), does not mention Jesus' death as a ransom but ends with the words "I am among you as one who serves" (cf. also John 13:4-17).

The early Christian interpretation of Jesus' death for others may be further elucidated by a comparison with the account of the death of Eleazar and that of the seven brothers and their mother in 2 Macc. 6:18-31; chapter 7 and in 4 Maccabees 5–7; 8–18. When King Antiochus compels the Jews to forsake the laws of their ancestors and no longer live by the laws of God, Eleazar refuses to eat swine's flesh, "welcoming death with honor rather than life with pollution" (2 Macc. 6:19) and leaving to the young "a noble example of how to die a good death willingly and nobly for the revered and holy laws" (v. 28). The seven brothers and their mother are tortured to death in the most cruel fashion because they are "ready to die rather than transgress the laws of their ancestors." They confront the king, who is depicted as personally presiding over the torture, with this message, and they comfort each other with the words "The Lord God is watching over us, and in truth has compassion over us, as Moses declared in his song that bore witness

26

against the people to their faces, when he said: 'And he will have compassion on his servants'" (2 Macc. 7:6, referring to Deut. 32:36).

These two Hellenistic-Jewish writings, which date from around 124 B.C.E. and from the end of the first century C.E. respectively, were strongly influenced by Greek, Hellenistic, and Roman ideas about dying for one's city or one's friends, for the law or for truth, and also about expiatory sacrifice to assuage the anger of the gods.[17] But that should not lead us to the all-too-simple conclusion that the ideas found there are illustrative only of the background of ideas concerning Jesus' death current in Hellenistic Christianity. In these two writings, Hellenistic conceptions are used to explain the death of martyrs obedient to the God of Israel, and there is no reason to assume a rigid separation between Palestinian and Hellenistic Judaism or between Palestinian and Hellenistic congregations in first-century Christianity.[18]

In 2 and 4 Maccabees the expressions "to die for" and "to give one's life for" are, above all, used in connection with the law. Eleazar is willing to die a good death "for the revered and holy laws" (2 Macc. 6:28), and the seven brothers "give up body and life for the law of our fathers" (2 Macc. 7:37). In 4 Maccabees the martyrs are said to have died "for the law" (6:27; 13:9), "for virtue's sake" (1:8), or "for the sake of reverence of God" (*eusebeia;* 9:6; 18:3). Many related expressions are found; all emphasize the martyrs' true obedience to God's commandments and their readiness to die rather than transgress any of them, even under the greatest pressure on the part of the tyrant.

Yet the martyrs in 2 Maccabees also share in the sins and the punishment of their people (7:18, 32). In 7:33 the last of the seven brothers to be martyred declares: "And if our living God is angry for a little while, to rebuke and discipline us, he will again be reconciled with his own servants." The effect of the death of the martyrs, in solidarity with Israel, is indeed that God is reconciled with his people (1:5; 5:20; 8:29) and that God's wrath turns into mercy. In 8:1-7 this is evident in the victories of Judas Maccabeus and his army of faithful Jews over the

---

17. For details, see J. W. van Henten, *The Maccabean Martyrs as Saviours of the Jewish People: A Study of 2 and 4 Maccabees* (JSJSup 57; Leiden: Brill, 1997); M. Hengel, *The Atonement: The Origins of the Doctrine in the New Testament* (London: SCM, 1981); and S. K. Williams, *Jesus' Death as Saving Event: The Background and Origin of a Concept* (HDR 2; Missoula, Mont.: Scholars Press, 1975).

18. So Hengel, *The Atonement*, 2-4, 60-61, against especially K. Wengst, *Christologische Formeln und Lieder des Urchristentums* (SNT 7; Gütersloh: Mohn, 1972).

enemy. In his last words the youngest brother prays for Israel, asking God "to show mercy soon to our nation . . . and through me and my brother to bring to an end the wrath of the Almighty which has justly fallen on our whole nation" (7:37-38).

As for the martyrs themselves, they will be vindicated by God; 2 Maccabees 7 repeatedly stresses their resurrection (vv. 9, 11, 14, 23, 29, 36). A bodily resurrection seems to be envisaged: the martyr expects to recover his tortured limbs through God (vv. 9; 14:46), and the mother expects to get her seven sons back in God's mercy (v. 29). At the same time there is reason to think that, like Onias and Jeremiah in 15:12-16, they will receive some form of existence in heaven (see 7:36). For the tyrant, the antagonist of God and his people, there will be no resurrection to life. He will not escape punishment (vv. 17, 19, 31, 34-37; chapter 9).

The martyrs in 4 Maccabees also receive eternal life after death, together with all God's faithful in the past, martyrs, near-martyrs, and people otherwise in distress, under the leadership of Abraham, Isaac, and Jacob (see, e.g., 7:18-19; 13:17; 18:23-24). The death of the martyrs has a direct impact on the land and the people (18:3-4). In 6:28-29 Eleazar dies, willingly, for the sake of *(dia)* the law. He prays to God: "Be merciful to your people and let our punishment be a satisfaction on their behalf (here we find *hyper* plus personal pronoun). Make my blood their purification, and take my life as a ransom for theirs."[19] The same idea recurs in 17:21, 22: "and the tyrant was punished and our land purified, since they became, as it were, a ransom for the sins of our nation.[20] Through the blood of these righteous ones and through the propitiation[21] of their death the divine providence rescued Israel, which had been shamefully treated."

In 2 and 4 Maccabees the death of the faithful Israelites brings about a decisive change for Israel.[22] The martyrs themselves are vindi-

---

19. *antipsychon autōn.*

20. Here again *antipsychon* is used, this time with the genitive *tēs tou ethnous hamartias.*

21. *tou hilastēriou;* cf. Rom. 3:25.

22. In some ways, the terminology of vicarious expiatory death in 4 Maccabees is more explicit than that in 2 Maccabees, but the underlying idea is the same. The relatively late date of 4 Maccabees does not preclude using it as a source of parallels for early Christian ideas, since the terms used in 4 Maccabees may be older than the writing itself. On the late date of 4 Maccabees, see van Henten, *The Maccabean Martyrs,* 73-81;

cated and exalted to live with God. They act and die as representatives of the people; therefore, Israel will benefit from the supreme loyalty to God that led them to their self-sacrifice.

Neither 2 Maccabees nor 4 Maccabees places this story in an eschatological context. At the end of 4 Maccabees (18:4) the nation lives in peace thanks to the martyrs, who are said to have restored the observance of the law *(eunomia)*. The emphasis, however, is on the fate of the martyrs themselves, who have demonstrated that those who obey the law recognize that devout reason is master of the passions — not only of the pains that come from within, but also of those that come from outside ourselves. Those who understood and followed this were deemed worthy of a divine inheritance (18:1-3).

In 2 Maccabees the deaths of Eleazar and of the seven brothers together with their mother mark a turning point in God's relationship with Israel — and, as a result, also in the military situation of Israel, so that, in the end, the temple is cleansed and temple worship restored. History has a way of repeating itself, however; the last battle mentioned in 2 Maccabees (chapter 15) is won after Razis has been martyred (2 Macc. 14:37-46).[23]

The analogy between the concept of Jesus' death for others and this view of the martyrs is evident; there are even agreements in terminology (compare, for instance, 2 Macc. 7:33, 37-38 with Rom. 5:6-11). But with Jesus' death the eschatological element comes in. Jesus has, in the eyes of his followers, a special position as inaugurator of a new era in God's dealings with humanity. In his case God's intervention proved not only decisive, but definitive.[24] This is expressed by those connected with Jesus in terms of forgiveness, reconciliation, redemption, and hope for salvation from the wrath of God's final judgment. Furthermore, it is not restricted to those who belong to Israel and truly obey God's commandment but includes all Jews and non-Jews who have placed their trust in Jesus as God's final envoy.

---

idem, "Datierung und Herkunft des vierten Makkabäersbuches," in J. W. van Henten et al., eds., *Tradition and Re-interpretation in Jewish and Early Christian Literature: Essays in Honour of Jürgen C. H. Lebram* (SPB 36; Leiden: Brill, 1986) 136-49.

23. See van Henten, *The Maccabean Martyrs*, 184-87.

24. Compare the voluntary death of Taxo and his seven sons in *Assumptio Mosis* 9, in order that their blood be avenged before the Lord. This is immediately followed by the appearance of God's kingdom throughout his whole creation in chapter 10. See on this pp. 49-53 below.

Jesus saw as his mission the inauguration of the definitive change inherent to the coming of God's kingdom. It is certainly possible and even probable that during his preaching in Galilee and Jerusalem, when his death had become a possibility to be reckoned with very seriously, Jesus, or Jesus' followers, considered this to be the death of a martyr, but decisive proof cannot be given. Whether they thought of his death in terms of the traditional material discussed in this section, we are not in a position to say. Most of what has been handed down about Jesus' own views of his death is found in the letters of Paul; nothing is found in Q (which never speaks explicitly about the meaning of Jesus' death), and only two closely related sayings are found in Mark (10:45 and 14:24). The second of these is bound up with the early Christian liturgy of the Lord's Supper, which may have influenced its transmission. The most we can say is that Jesus, convinced of the speedy and complete realization of God's kingdom and of his own vindication after his death, may have regarded his death as serving God's purpose. In what terms he expressed this, we do not know for certain.[25]

The Influence of the Fourth Servant Song in Isaiah

In the attempt to determine Jesus' own attitude toward his death, a question that has received considerable attention should be assessed briefly here. It involves the possible influence of the Fourth Servant Song in Isa. 52:13–53:12 on early Christian interpretation of the death of Jesus and, according to many, also on Jesus' own view of his impending death.

A few decades ago it had become "almost an axiom of . . . New Testament study that most of the New Testament writers, and probably our Lord himself, were controlled in their christological thinking by the

---

25. See also Schürmann, "Jesu ureigenes Todesverständnis," in *Gottes Reich — Jesu Geschick*, esp. 198-223. N. A. Dahl considers it probable that "Jesus not only foresaw his own death, but actually ascribed to it a vicarious significance and saw it as a necessary presupposition for the coming of the kingdom of God (*Jesus the Christ: The Historical Origins of Christological Doctrine* [ed. D. H. Juel; Minneapolis: Fortress, 1991] 100).

figure of the Suffering Servant of the Lord."[26] In this respect the work of Joachim Jeremias was very influential,[27] as was that of Oscar Cullmann, who devoted a chapter of his *Christology of the New Testament* to "Jesus the Suffering Servant of God."[28] T. W. Manson, who saw a strong connection between the notions Son of Man and Servant of the Lord in Jesus' life and thought, should be mentioned here as well.[29] Today, however, many scholars are of the opinion that the importance of the idea of the suffering servant for early Christianity has been greatly overrated; moreover, it is difficult to demonstrate that Jesus himself interpreted his destiny in light of this passage from scripture. This has been shown convincingly by C. K. Barrett in an important contribution to the memorial volume for T. W. Manson[30] and by Morna D. Hooker in her *Jesus and the Servant*. Whoever may be envisaged in the Fourth Servant Song (the righteous in Israel or the prophet or both), a decisive turn in the fate of God's servant is announced. In Isa. 53:1-10 the servant's sufferings unto death are described at great length and interpreted as sufferings on behalf of the sins of others (see vv. 4-6, 10, 12). Interestingly, this interpretation of suffering stands apart in Old Testament literature, and with regard to its influence on later texts Martin Hengel has pointed out that "so far . . . we have no clear text from

26. So C. K. Barrett in his Foreword (p. ix) to Morna D. Hooker, *Jesus and the Servant: The Influence of the Servant Concept of Deutero-Isaiah in the New Testament* (London: SPCK, 1959).

27. J. Jeremias, *"Pais Theou," TWNT* 5 (1954) 676-713 = *TDNT* 5 (1967) 677-717; cf. the reworked article *"Pais Theou im Neuen Testament,"* in *Abba: Studien zur neutestamentlichen Theologie und Zeitgeschichte* (Göttingen: Vandenhoeck & Ruprecht, 1966) 191-216. Compare his *New Testament Theology: The Proclamation of Jesus* (New York: Charles Scribner's Sons, 1971) §24.ii, "The Interpretation of Suffering," 286-99, translation of *Neutestamentliche Theologie I. Teil: Die Verkündigung Jesu* (Gütersloh: Mohn, 1971) §24.ii, "Die Leidensdeutung," 272-84.

28. O. Cullmann, *The Christology of the New Testament* (Philadelphia: Westminster, 1959) 51-82, translation of *Die Christologie des Neuen Testaments* (Tübingen: Mohr Siebeck, 1957) 50-81. For further advocates of this view, see Hooker, *Jesus and the Servant,* 1-24; and H. Haag, *Der Gottesknecht bei Deuterojesaja* (Darmstadt: Wissenschaftliche Buchgesellschaft, 1985) 66-79.

29. T. W. Manson, *The Servant-Messiah: A Study of the Public Ministry of Jesus* (Cambridge: Cambridge University Press, 1950) 72-74.

30. C. K. Barrett, "The Background of Mark 10:45," in A. J. B. Higgins, ed., *New Testament Essays: Studies in Memory of T. W. Manson, 1893-1958* (Manchester: Manchester University Press, 1959) 1-18. See also Barrett, *Jesus and the Gospel Tradition,* 39-41.

pre-Christian Judaism which speaks of the vicarious suffering of the Messiah in connection with Isa. 53."[31]

This, of course, does not exclude the possibility that early Christians did use this passage. In fact, Hengel (who aims at restoring the balance after recent neglect of Isaiah 53) is firmly convinced that Isaiah 53 had an influence on the origin and shaping of the earliest kerygma. He says: "Neither the formula of the 'surrender' of Jesus nor that of his representative dying 'for many' or 'for us' would have come into being without the background of this mysterious prophecy."[32] The suffering servant of Isa. 50:4-11 and Isa. 52:13–53:12 certainly could provide a suitable model for the explanation of Jesus' life, death, and vindication. The person portrayed here is an ideal servant of the Lord, a prophetic figure speaking on God's behalf against God's and his own adversaries, ready to suffer. This servant resembles the other prophetic envoys rejected by Israel and is one of the suffering righteous ones. He is closely related to those martyrs who refused to buckle under tyrants and died rather than transgress God's commandments. No doubt these two passages — particularly the second, with its emphasis on exaltation after humiliation and the attention paid to the effects of the servant's sufferings for others — could have served very well the purpose of those who wanted to determine the meaning of Jesus' death.

However, notwithstanding Jeremias's careful listing of all the possible references and allusions to the texts, words, phrases, and ideas found Isa. 52:13–53:12 in the writings of the New Testament, the evidence for the use of this passage in early Christianity is slight. In Acts 8:32-33 the Ethiopian eunuch reads Isa. 53:7-8, and in vv. 34-36 Philip explains to him that the prophet is referring to Jesus. The hymn in 1 Peter 2:21-25, inserted in an exhortatory context, incorporates phrases from the Deutero-Isaianic passage. But both these texts are late. The use of the designation "the servant of the Lord" in Matt. 12:18-21 (quoting Isa. 42:1-4 in a special form) does not necessarily evoke the image of the *suffering* servant of Isaiah 53, and the same is true of this expression in Acts 3:13, 26.

Next there are stray quotations, of Isa. 52:15 in Rom. 15:21; of 53:1 in Rom. 10:16; and of 53:4 in Matt. 8:17. In no instance is there any reference to vicarious suffering. The last quotation, "he took our

---

31. Hengel, *The Atonement*, 59.
32. Ibid.

infirmities and bore our diseases," refers to Jesus' healings and his exorcisms. Only in the Lukan passion narrative do we find a reference to Isa. 53:12, "He was numbered with the transgressors" (22:37). In the earlier material we find that the use of the term "many" in Mark 10:45 and 14:24 is often thought to have been influenced by Isa. 53:11-12, but it is very difficult to prove this conclusively. On the other hand, it is likely that the wording of Rom. 4:25 was influenced by Isa. 53:12 LXX, but here we have a particular, probably Pauline variant of the more general surrender formula.[33]

All in all, we must conclude that the influence of Isa. 52:13–53:12 on the earliest Christian kerygma can hardly be demonstrated. A fortiori, there is no proof that Jesus himself was profoundly or uniquely influenced by this scriptural passage.

Conclusion

The three models of interpretation of Jesus' death found in the earliest layers of traditional material can all provide some insight into Jesus' own understanding of his life and death, as well as into the christology of his earliest followers. Jesus may have interpreted rejection and possible death as that of God's final envoy to Israel. It is also possible that he saw himself as an obedient suffering servant who would be vindicated by God. It is impossible to say with certainty whether Jesus regarded his death as a dying for others, along the lines of martyrdom found in 2 and 4 Maccabees, but it is certainly possible that he did so.

In all instances the early Christian models of interpretation take for granted that Jesus' death was that of one who was related to God in a unique way and that it brought about a definitive and lasting change in the relationship between God and those faithful to him. Jesus' death, followed by his vindication and exaltation, had inaugurated a new era. This conviction connected the christology that developed after Easter with the eschatology proclaimed before Easter.

---

33. On this, see also de Jonge, *Christology in Context*, 179-81; idem, "Jesus' Death for Others," 146. Schürmann, *Gottes Reich — Jesu Geschick*, 236-41, also comes to a negative conclusion.

CHAPTER 3

Jesus' Message about the Kingdom of God

In the first two chapters it has become clear that already before his death Jesus was regarded by his disciples as an eschatological figure who had inaugurated the fervently expected new era in God's dealings with Israel and the world. The eschatological convictions intrinsically linked with the early Christian preaching about Jesus' death and resurrection can only be explained if we assume this to have been the case.

The three models used to interpret his violent death are also found in contemporary Jewish writings, as we have seen. Typically Christian is the conviction that Jesus was a prophet, a righteous one, and a martyr who by his death and vindication brought about a definitive change in the history of the world; in other words, the time of the end had already begun in what happened to him.

The conviction that God had vindicated Jesus by raising him from the dead, central for the Christian faith, need not carry with it the notion that the end time had already begun. The fact that the Jesus community after Easter believed that the definitive turn had taken place can only be explained by assuming that already before Jesus' death his followers believed that their master had inaugurated the new era promised by God.

If this is so, the words about the kingdom of God attributed to Jesus are very important indeed. A general survey of the words on the kingdom of God in our oldest written sources, the letters of Paul, Mark, and Q, is in order.

Paul on the Kingdom of God

In 1 Thess. 2:11-12 Paul describes his activity as an apostle as that of a father guiding his children. "We exhorted each one of you and encouraged you and charged you to lead a life worthy of God, who calls you to his kingdom and glory." Paul's preaching of the gospel promises those who accept it a share in the final salvation, designated as God's glorious kingdom, and his exhortations prepare them for their participation in it. For Paul the arrival of the kingdom coincides with the parousia of Christ, mentioned five times in 1 Thessalonians (1:10; 2:19; 3:13; 4:15-17; 5:23), but he never explicitly connects the two events. He does stress, however, in a way comparable to that found in 2:11-12, that the lives of the believers should be directed at the parousia (3:12-13; 5:23) with the help of the Lord. In a well-known passage (4:13-18) he assures his readers that all believers will share in the new life to be granted at Christ's imminent parousia, including both those who have died in the meantime and those who, like Paul himself, will be alive at the time.

What Paul says in this early letter is also found elsewhere. I briefly point to his conviction that the unrighteous will not inherit the kingdom of God: see his specifications of wrong behavior in 1 Cor. 6:9-10 and Gal. 5:19-21. Next, there are his statements concerning the resurrection in 1 Corinthians 15. He emphasizes that "flesh and blood cannot inherit the kingdom of God" (15:50; cf. vv. 51-57), and he explicitly connects the realization of God's final kingly rule with the parousia. After destroying every rule and authority and power, Christ will hand over the kingdom to the Father (15:23-28).

For Paul the kingdom of God is directly connected with Jesus' imminent return in glory. In two texts, however, he speaks of the presence of the kingdom in the community of believers, thanks to the display of the power of God in the Spirit. "The kingdom of God does not consist in talk but in power" (1 Cor. 4:20); "the kingdom of God does not mean food and drink but righteousness and peace and joy in the Holy Spirit" (Rom. 14:17).[1]

There are many points of agreement between Paul's statements

---

1. For Paul, the activity of the Holy Spirit is a sign of the approaching definitive realization of God's promises: Rom. 8:1-27; 1 Cor. 12:1-13; 2 Cor. 3:1-18; 5:5; Gal. 4:4-6; 5:5, 13-26.

concerning the kingdom of God and those found in Mark and Q. The chief difference lies in the fact that nearly all the statements found in Mark and Q are attributed to Jesus himself. Paul very seldom refers to words and acts of Jesus,[2] so it is not surprising that he did not connect his (sometimes stereotyped, and therefore probably traditional) preaching about the kingdom with the earthly Jesus either. But Mark and Q do; on the basis of their testimony, we may regard the message of the kingdom of God as a vital part of Jesus' preaching.

Kingdom Sayings in Mark and Q as Evidence for Jesus' Own Message

Let us, therefore, briefly review the most important sayings of Jesus about the kingdom, concentrating on those in Mark and Q. It seems to me that together they present a coherent picture. Although we can never be certain that individual words were spoken by Jesus as our oldest sources record them, it is extremely plausible that the overall picture is reliable.

According to Q Jesus taught his disciples to pray "Father, hallowed be thy name; thy kingdom come" (Luke 11:2).[3] They are to pray for a new initiative by God, a new era in which God receives the honor due to him. God is called Father, a form of address characteristic of the early Christian community (Gal. 4:6-7; Rom. 8:14-16) and of Jesus (Mark 14:36; Luke 10:21-22, par. Matt. 11:25-27). It is generally considered to go back to Jesus' confidence in his unique relationship to God.[4] This beginning of the Lord's Prayer may be connected with another section about prayer in Q (Luke 11:9-13, par. Matt. 7:7-11) ending with the words "If you, who are evil, know how to give good gifts to your children, how much more will your heavenly Father give good things (so Matthew; Luke has "the Holy Spirit") to those who ask him," and with yet another Q pericope (Luke 12:22-31, par. Matt. 6:25-33), which urges

---

2. On this, see M. de Jonge, *Christology in Context: The Earliest Christian Response to Jesus* (Philadelphia: Westminster, 1988) 87-88.

3. Cf. Matt. 6:9-10. The shorter text in Luke is more likely to represent the text of Q.

4. See below Chapter 8, pp. 106-9.

believers to trust God completely: "your Father knows that you need these things. Instead, seek his kingdom, and these things shall be yours as well" (Luke 12:30b-31).

The kingdom of God will bring a complete change on earth. The four beatitudes which, in all probability, formed the beginning of Jesus' preaching in Q make this very clear (Luke 6:20-23; cf. Matt. 5:3, 6, 4, 11-12). The first three are addressed to the poor ("for yours is the kingdom of God"),[5] to those who hunger, and to those who weep, but the fourth is directed to Jesus' followers who are hated and reviled because of Jesus. Other words about the kingdom are also oriented towards the disciples.

As in Paul, certain sayings in the Synoptic Gospels deal with the ethical requirements for receiving a share in God's kingdom. Contrary to those mentioned by Paul, they are very radical. So, for example, Mark 9:47, "And if your eye causes you to sin, pluck it out; it is better for you to enter the kingdom of God with one eye than with two eyes to be thrown into hell." Or read the story about the rich man who, in order to inherit eternal life, has to sell everything he possesses, and to give to the poor and follow Jesus (Mark 10:17-31, par. Matt. 19:16-30; Luke 18: 18-30). Followers of Jesus are indeed sent out "carrying no purse, no bag and no sandals" (Luke 10:4; see 1-12, par. Matt. 9:37–10:16).[6] Another word of Jesus makes clear that one has to receive the kingdom of God as a child receives a present, utterly without pretensions, in order to enter it (Mark 10:13-16, par. Luke 18:15-17; cf. Matt. 19:13-15; 18:3).[7] This group of sayings presupposes a radical interpretation of God's will, generally considered to be typical of Jesus, who always asks for the real intention of the commandments of the Torah and who critically reviews the rules of men based upon them.[8]

---

5. Cf. James 2:5.

6. Cf. also Luke 9:57-62, mainly consisting of Q texts: family duties, such as burying one's father, have to give way to following the Son of Man. On wandering preachers, see G. Theissen, *Studien zur Soziologie des Urchristentums* (WUNT 19; Tübingen: Mohr Siebeck, 1979) esp. 79-141, 201-31.

7. Other related texts are Mark 12:34 (and also 15:43?); Luke 13:24, par. Matt. 7:13-14; Matt. 7:21; 25:21, 23, 34; Acts 14:22; John 3:3, 5. Matthew 16:19 speaks about the keys of the kingdom entrusted to Peter; in 23:13 Jesus reproaches the scribes and the Pharisees for having shut the kingdom of heaven against others, and not entering it themselves (cf. Luke 11:52).

8. See E. P. Sanders, *Jesus and Judaism* (London: SCM, 1985), especially 245-69.

An important image for the coming kingdom is that of a banquet. A Q saying (Luke 13:28-29, par. Matt. 8:11-12) speaks about a feast in the kingdom of God where many people, coming from all the corners of the earth, will sit down together with Abraham, Isaac, and Jacob. Woe to those who will find themselves excluded![9] In the description of the Last Supper in Mark 14:22-25 we find a related saying: "Truly I say to you, I shall not drink again of the fruit of the vine until that day I drink it new in the kingdom of God" (v. 25).[10] The wine symbolizes the joy of the kingdom in which Jesus will share; the kingdom is clearly expected to arrive in the near future. I would suggest that this promise of a future feast with unexpected guests may be connected with the stories of Jesus' meals with tax collectors and other men and women who were not reckoned among the righteous (Mark 2:14-17, par. Matt. 9:9-13; Luke 5:27-32; and Luke 7:34, par. Matt. 11:19; cf. Luke 15:1; 19:1-10). A saying found only in Matt. 21:31 fits here admirably: "Truly I say to you, the tax collectors and harlots go into the kingdom before you."

In Mark and Q is this future kingdom ever connected with the parousia? As far as I can see, this is the case only in Mark 9:1, which follows 8:38, and this connection has to be attributed to Mark's redactional activity. Mark 8:38 speaks about the Son of Man coming in glory with the holy angels; in 9:1 Jesus declares: "Truly, I say to you, there are some standing here who will not taste death before they see the kingdom of God come with power."[11] Mark 8:38 is to be linked with 13:26 and 14:62; the notion of the future coming of the Son of Man figures prominently in a number of sayings of Jesus. I consider it likely that Jesus himself used a veiled reference to "one like a son of man" in Dan. 7:13-14 in order to define his own mission.[12] The saying in Mark 9:1 emphasizing that the kingdom will come during the lifetime of at least

9. In Luke the "workers of iniquity" (v. 27) are excluded. Matthew speaks of "the sons of the kingdom," that is, the official Israel that rejects Jesus (cf. 21:43-46). In this connection, Luke 22:28-30, par. Matt. 19:28 may also be mentioned. In the version of the saying found in Luke, Jesus speaks of the eating and drinking of the disciples in his kingdom. See also Luke 14:15, 16-24, par. Matt. 22:1-14.

10. Cf. Luke 22:15-18 and the reference to the coming of the Lord in Paul's account of the Last Supper in 1 Cor. 11:23-26. See also below, pp. 61-62.

11. Matt. 16:27-28 speaks of the coming of the Son of Man, in the glory of the Father and "in his kingdom." See also Matt. 20:21, which reads "in your kingdom" instead of "in your glory" (Mark 10:37). See, again, below pp. 77-79.

12. See below, Chapter 7.

some of the followers present may also very well go back to Jesus.[13] Only later were the notions of parousia and kingdom of God directly connected, by Mark and by Paul in 1 Corinthians — though, as we have seen, Paul did not do this in his earlier letter, 1 Thessalonians.

The collection of sayings in Mark and Q discussed so far shows a remarkable coherence. At several points a connection may be made with words of Jesus that can otherwise be established to belong to the core of his mission; so we are allowed to conclude that these sayings about the kingdom represent Jesus' stand on the matter.

God's Rule, Future and Present

There is still a last group of important sayings, which speak about the coming of the kingdom of God in connection with Jesus' mission in the present. As is well known, they have provoked an enormous discussion in this century, particularly in connection with C. H. Dodd's interpretation of them in his *The Parables of the Kingdom* of 1935.[14] There is no need to repeat here the various points of view; let me just try to indicate the main issues involved. Mark characterizes Jesus' mission by means of the first words spoken by Jesus in his Gospel: "The time is fulfilled, and the kingdom of God is near; repent and believe in the gospel" (1:15). The same message is found in Q, where it is to be announced by Jesus' disciples sent out to preach and to heal: "The kingdom of God has come near to you" (Luke 10:9, par. Matt. 10:7 [without "to you"]).[15] The Greek verb used here should be interpreted as "is at hand."[16] The kingdom is not yet present, but

13. See also Mark 13:30 — "Truly, I say to you, this generation will not pass away before all these things take place." This saying may not be played off against the earlier saying, as if these two texts represent two different stages in the short-term expectation of the kingdom. "This generation" refers to "all that are alive" without envisaging each person in that category individually.

14. A revised edition (London: Nisbet, 1936) was reprinted many times.

15. Cf. Luke 10:11; 9:2. Mark 6:7, 12-13 refer (implicitly) to Mark 1:15, but mention only the preaching of repentance.

16. See the parallel use of the term in Matt. 26:45; Luke 21:8, 20; Rom. 13:12; James 5:8; 1 Pet. 4:7. The expression "the kingdom of God (or: of heaven) is at hand" is found also in the clearly redactional passages Matt. 3:2; Luke 10:11; 21:31.

it has drawn so near that it is all-important for those who hear the message. Hence Mark's "the time is fulfilled" and "repent, and believe in the gospel."

A Q saying (Luke 11:20, par. Matt. 12:28) goes one step farther. In one of Jesus' replies to the remark that he casts out demons by Beelzebul, the prince of demons, he says: "But if it is by the finger of God that I cast out demons, then the kingdom of God has come upon you."[17] The battle between God and Satan has already begun. In what follows Satan is compared to a strong man guarding his own palace, but defeated by one who is stronger than he. The same image is found in the parallel passage in Mark 3:22-27, where the expression "kingdom of God" does not occur, but Jesus' activity in destroying Satan's kingdom receives a similar emphasis: "How can Satan cast out Satan? If a kingdom is divided against itself, that kingdom cannot stand" (vv. 23-24).

The kingdom of God is at hand; Jesus announces it and calls for repentance. His radical ethic has to be understood in this context. In his healing of the diseased, his exorcisms, his concern for those who are on the wrong way, his offer of a new perspective to the poor and the distressed, and his assurance to all that God as a Father will hear their prayer, he not only announces the kingdom but also inaugurates it. This is also borne out by the difficult Q saying Luke 16:16, par. Matt. 11:12-13 about the kingdom coming violently,[18] and by the parable of the mustard seed found in Mark and Q (Mark 4:31-33; Luke 13:18-19, par. Matt. 13:31-32) and the accompanying parables in Mark 4:26-29 and in Q (Luke 13:20-21, par. Matt. 13:33).[19] In all texts belonging to this last group the emphasis is on the complete breakthrough of the kingdom of God in the near future, and the radical definitive change resulting from it. But this event is even more eagerly awaited because the dynamic presence of the kingdom is

17. Cf. Exod. 8:19. Matthew reads "by the Spirit of God."

18. The differences between Luke and Matthew make reconstruction of the original Q saying a hazardous undertaking. I think that *biazetai* in Matthew is more likely to be original than *euaggelizetai* in Luke; in the second half of the saying, Matthew gives an explanation of what is found in Luke (who is therefore probably nearer to Q). *Biazetai* should twice be interpreted as a middle form; it is used *in bonam partem*.

19. See in Mark also the parable of the sower and its interpretation (4:3-9, 14-20) and the typically Markan verse 4:11, "To you has been given the secret of the kingdom of God, but for those outside everything is in parables."

already manifest in Jesus' message and actions — at least for those who hear and see and accept it.[20]

In emphasizing this I find myself in agreement with the views of a great majority of scholars.[21] It has become clear that for Jesus and his Jewish contemporaries (to quote Graham N. Stanton) "the kingdom of God is God's kingly rule, the time and place where God's power and will hold sway."[22] Many scholars will agree with Stanton's remark that this rule has a future and a present aspect and is concerned with God's initiative as well as with the individual's response. Referring to the dispute between those who with Johannes Weiss (and Albert Schweitzer) emphasized Jesus' insistence on God's all-overpowering initiative in the near future and the followers of C. H. Dodd, who claimed that for Jesus the kingdom of God had actually come with his own actions and words, Stanton remarks: "Over the past fifty years many scholars have rejected both these approaches and have tried to plot a middle path: Jesus proclaimed that the kingdom was in some ways partly present in his actions and his teaching (or was already making its impact felt in the present), though its full and final disclosure still lay in the future."[23] One should speak of the *dynamic presence* of God's kingly rule in the words and actions of Jesus, determining the faith, hope, and way of life of his followers.[24]

20. Cf. the statement in Mark 10:14, "for to such belongs the kingdom of God," which is followed by the expression "to enter it (the kingdom)" in the next verse; cf. also Luke 6:20, par. Matt. 5:3, "for yours is the kingdom of God," alongside Luke 6:21, par. Matt. 5:6, 4, "you shall be satisfied" and "you shall laugh." See also the texts in which Paul establishes a connection between the future kingdom and the present community (Rom. 14:17 and 1 Cor. 4:20).

21. A number of scholars who rely heavily on the *Gospel of Thomas* are of a different opinion. Because this work does not show interest in the future breakthrough of the kingdom of God, they regard the sayings in the Synoptics about the future kingdom of God as secondary. Not only do they reach this conclusion on the basis of a wrong assessment of the available material, but they also disregard basic notions in the Jewish understanding of God's sovereign rule (see Chapter 4 below) and wrongly assume a complete break, not only between Jesus and John the Baptist (and other contemporary prophetic figures) but also between Jesus and his followers after Easter.

22. G. N. Stanton, *The Gospels and Jesus* (Oxford: Oxford University Press, 1989) 196.

23. Ibid., 191-92.

24. So also H. Merklein, *Jesu Botschaft von der Gottesherrschaft* (SBS 111; 3d ed. Stuttgart: Katholisches Bibelwerk, 1989) 65, on Luke 11:20 (a central text for the proponents of "realized eschatology"): "Lk 11,20 schliesst die futurische Dimension der

I add here a number of clear and forceful statements of Leander E. Keck in his discussion with Bultmann and his pupils in his *A Future for the Historical Jesus*, a book already referred to in Chapter 1. Over against existential hermeneutics concentrating on the response of human individuals and shifting the discussion from "future" to "futurity" as a mode of the present, he emphasizes that "the kingship of God is that state of affairs in which the entire creation adequately reflects the will of God" (p. 222). It is essentially future: "the kingdom's coming in God's own time implies the judgment of God upon the present. The news that the kingdom is accessible now is good news because it offers proleptic participation in it for those who trust the news and its herald" (pp. 222-23). Jesus "lived and worked out of the future into the present, and in so doing reconstituted it as the beachhead of the future" (p. 223). If we take this seriously we will not expect ideological or complete ethical consistency in Jesus. We cannot eliminate a priori particular aspects of the perplexing variety in the picture of Jesus' words and actions handed down to us. Referring to the earlier discussion on what was distinctive or characteristic of Jesus, Keck declares "holding all these dimensions of his career together was precisely what was characteristic of Jesus" (p. 224).

Jesus' Kingdom Sayings and Other Elements in His Preaching

If this was the main thrust of Jesus' proclamation of God's rule as king, and if this proclamation constituted the core of his preaching, a number of questions arise:

First, if Jesus' insistence on the speedy future manifestation of the kingdom of God as well as on its dynamic presence in his own words and actions was characteristic of him, we may ask whether there are parallels to this in other contemporary Jewish writings.

Gottesherrschaft keineswegs aus, sondern bekommt unter dieser Voraussetzung erst seine eigene Brisanz. Hier wird vielmehr deutlich, dass die Gottesherrschaft für Jesus ein dynamischer Begriff ist, der ein *Geschehen* anzeigt, in dem die eschatologische Zukunft bereits die Gegenwart erfasst." Cf. also G. R. Beasley-Murray, *Jesus and the Kingdom of God* (Grand Rapids: Eerdmans; Exeter: Paternoster, 1986) 338: "The decisive shift from eschatology of the future alone to the future-in-the-present was the work of Jesus, not of Paul and John."

Another important question is how Jesus' preaching about the kingdom of God was related to his view of his suffering, death, and vindication by God. One thing seems certain: he experienced rejection and opposition and must have reckoned with the prospect of a violent death.[25] His message about the kingdom implies that he was convinced that God would vindicate him. His message about the complete breakthrough of God's sovereign rule in the near future would be proven true; he and his followers would have a share in it. It is difficult to make out how he saw the relationship between his vindication and the complete realization of God's rule.

Third, the fact that Jesus assigned to himself a central role in the coming of God's rule on earth, not only as a herald but as one who inaugurated it, implies a christology. To what extent did this lead to the use of explicit christological designations in the circle of his disciples during his wanderings in Galilee and Judea, or in his own views about his mission?

These questions will receive due attention in the following chapters. The first is one of the topics dealt with in the next chapter, where we shall compare Jesus' message about the kingdom of God with contemporary ideas about God's sovereign rule on earth. The complicated second question will be treated in Chapters 5–7. Finally, Chapter 8 will connect the preaching about the kingdom of God to the notions "Messiah" and "Son of God."

---

25. On this, see above, Chapter 2, pp. 18-23.

CHAPTER 4

Contemporary Ideas about
the Kingdom of God

It is useful to compare the statements about God's kingdom in the earliest Christian sources with contemporary Jewish ideas about God's kingship and rule. Odo Camponovo has recently given a very useful survey of those ideas, studying them in the contexts of the writings in which they occur and emphasizing their variety.[1] He rightly remarks that there is no such thing as a Jewish doctrine of the kingdom of God; moreover, the theme of God's kingship, in the present and the future, is certainly not a major one in Jewish literature, as it is not in the Hebrew Bible or in the Septuagint. God is king and his rule will be fully manifested in the future. This much is certain. But the faithful who meditate upon it and write about it come up with a great many associations and images. Where these are combined with pictures of God's definitive intervention in the future, apocalyptic and otherwise, the result is again a great variety of statements and images. The best we can do is to compare individual Jewish texts with individual Christian ones, particularly those which are most likely to represent Jesus' own views, and ask what light the Jewish texts shed on the early Christian ones. In doing so we may find that such comparisons not

---

1. O. Camponovo, *Königtum, Königsherrschaft und Reich Gottes in den früh-jüdischen Schriften* (OBO 58; Freiburg: Universitätsverlag; Göttingen: Vandenhoeck & Ruprecht, 1984). Camponovo sees it as his task to present the Jewish material and so does not relate it to the statements found in Christian sources. See also the essays in Martin Hengel and Anna Maria Schwemer, eds., *Königsherrschaft und himmlischer Kult im Judentum und in der hellenistischen Welt* (WUNT 55; Tübingen: Mohr Siebeck, 1991).

only yield analogies, but also bring to light points that are typical for early Christianity.

The Psalms of Solomon

Let us start by reviewing some interesting features of the *Psalms of Solomon,* a Jewish writing from Palestine, the final version of which is commonly dated about 45-40 B.C.E. These psalms, stemming from pious, law-abiding circles in and around Jerusalem, praise God's kingship in a number of places. The second psalm, looking back on Pompey's ignominious death, describes his pride and self-exaltation in contrast to the genuine might of God.

> He said: I will be lord of land and sea;
> And he did not recognize that God is great,
> Mighty in his great strength.
> He is king in the heavens,
> And judges kings and dominions.
> It is he who raises me up to glory,
> And lays low the proud in eternal destruction, in dishonor,
> Because they knew him not.
> And now, behold, princes of the earth, the judgment of the Lord.
> For he is a great king, and righteous, judging the earth that is
> under heaven. (vv. 29-32)[2]

Psalm 17 stresses that God is king for ever. It begins: "Lord, you yourself are our king for ever and ever" (v. 1) and ends with the proclamation: "The Lord himself is our king for ever and ever" (v. 46).[3] Based on this conviction is the firm expectation that God will intervene shortly and

---

2. The translation is adapted from that of S. P. Brock in H. F. D. Sparks, *The Apocryphal Old Testament* (Oxford: Clarendon, 1984) 657.

3. My translation, as given in M. de Jonge, ed., *Outside the Old Testament* (Cambridge: Cambridge University Press, 1985) 168-75. See also my article "The Expectation of the Future in the Psalms of Solomon," *Neotestamentica* 23 (1989) 93-117, now in M. de Jonge, *Jewish Eschatology, Early Christian Christology, and the Testaments of the Twelve Patriarchs: Collected Essays* (NovTSup 63; Leiden: Brill, 1991) 3-27. In references to this essay in the following notes, the page numbers are from this volume.

bring a change in the fate of Israel by sending a king from the family of David.

> We shall hope in God, our savior,
> For the might of our God is for ever with mercy,
> and the kingdom of our God is for ever over the nations
>   in judgment.
> You, O Lord, chose David as king over Israel,
> And you swore to him concerning his seed for ever,
> That his kingship would never fail before you. (vv. 3-4)

There is a natural connection between God's kingship in the present, demonstrated in his judgment on his enemies and his mercy and help for those who obey him (see, e.g., *Ps. Sol.* 2:33-37), and the final demonstration of his rule, expected in the near future by the pious in distress. In one case, *Ps. Sol.* 5:18-19, it is not even clear whether the present or the future is in view. The most likely translation of these verses is:

> Those who fear the Lord rejoice in good things,
> In your royal rule your goodness is on Israel.
> Blessed is the glory of the Lord, for he is king.

Many commentators, however, follow von Gebhardt's suggestion that the indicative should be changed to an optative, thus bringing the ending of this psalm into line with that of other psalms (4:24; 11:8; 12:4-6; cf. 17:45-46; 18:5). If that proposal is accepted, v. 18 originally spoke about the future: "May those who fear the Lord rejoice. . . . Let your goodness be on Israel in your royal rule."[4]

Psalm 17, then, speaks about the definitive manifestation of the rule of God, the king, in the actions of the awaited king from the seed

---

4. The standard edition remains that of O. von Gebhardt, *Psalmoi Solomōntos: Die Psalmen Salomos zum ersten Male mit Benutzung der Athoshandschrift und des Codex Casanatensis herausgegeben* (TU 13/2; Leipzig: Hinrichs, 1895), but see now R. R. Hann, *The Manuscript History of the Psalms of Solomon* (SBLSCS 13; Chico, Calif.: Scholars Press, 1982). Von Gebhardt changed *euphranthēsan* to *euphrantheiēsan*. On this matter see O. Camponovo, *Königtum*, 216-18, who lists the opinions of various other commentators. S. P. Brock in *The Apocryphal Old Testament* follows von Gebhardt; R. B. Wright in J. H. Charlesworth, ed., *The Old Testament Pseudepigrapha*, vol. 2 (Garden City, N.Y.: Doubleday, 1985) retains the text of the manuscripts.

of David. Here (and in a somewhat different way in *Ps. Sol.* 18)[5] the heavenly king acts through an earthly representative. We should note, however, that elsewhere in this writing the future intervention of God is anticipated without human intermediaries (7:10; 8:27-31; 9:8-11; 10:5-8; 11; 12:6; 14:9-10; 15:12-13). For the expectation of these psalms it is essential that God prove his mercy and his power by intervening in the course of events, but it is not essential that he use an ideal Davidic king or someone else appointed by him.[6] The *Psalms of Solomon* are, in this respect, representative of Jewish expectation in general.

The prophecy of Nathan to David recorded in 2 Sam. 7:4-17 (esp. vv. 11-14) and the many Old Testament texts related to it lie at the basis of the expectation of the Davidic king in *Ps. Sol.* 17.[7] This is evident in v. 4, already quoted, as well as in v. 21:

> Behold, O Lord, and raise up unto them their king, the son of
> David,
> At the time you have (fore)seen, to rule over Israel your servant.

We may also mention v. 32:

> He (will be) a righteous king over them, instructed by God,
> And there is no unrighteousness among them in his days.
> For all are holy, and their king an anointed (of the) Lord.[8]

The activities of this king are described in vv. 21-44. Many Old Testament themes and texts are alluded to, and a very variegated and not always consistent picture is the result.[9] This anointed son of David is not only a

---

5. On this see de Jonge, "The Expectation," p. 10 and n. 27.
6. Ibid., 11.
7. Ibid., 10.
8. On the difficulties in this verse, see ibid., pp. 10, 14-15, and n. 25.
9. For details, see ibid., 8-13 and also the notes on my translation of *Psalms of Solomon* 17 in *Outside the Old Testament*. J. Schüpphaus has tried to distinguish two redactions of this psalm, the first speaking about a Davidic king saving Israel in distress, the second presenting the picture of a holy, wise, and fully obedient servant of God governing a holy people; see J. Schüpphaus, *Die Psalmen Salomos* (AGJU 7; Leiden: Brill, 1977) especially 64-73. Whereas it is quite likely that the *Psalms of Solomon* received their present form during a period of intensive use, I consider it unlikely that we shall ever be able to retrace their literary history in detail.

warrior who destroys God's enemies and purges Jerusalem from the nations in order to make a place for "the tribes of the people made holy by the Lord its God" (so v. 26). In accordance with Deut. 17:16-17,

> He will not put his trust in horse and rider and bow,
> Nor will he multiply for himself gold and silver for war. (v. 33)

In fact, he will be a perfect servant of God:

> The Lord himself is his king, the hope of him who is strong through hope in God. (v. 34; cf. v. 39)

Further,

> His words are more refined than the finest gold,
> In the assemblies will he judge the tribes of a sanctified people.
> His words are as the words of holy ones in the midst of sanctified peoples. (v. 43)

In the overall picture of the anointed one presented in *Psalms of Solomon* 17, the spiritual aspects dominate (see also v. 37, referring to Isa. 11:1-5). He will govern over a holy people. Everything centers on Israel and Jerusalem, but the essential thing is that all men and women serve God in righteousness and holiness under the king's leadership.

Here the final manifestation of God's rule takes place through the good offices of a Davidic king, "an anointed of the Lord" who remains completely dependent on God. In *Psalms of Solomon* 17 the spiritual side of his rule is strongly emphasized. In the early Christian view of the kingdom of God, it is therefore not at all strange for the kingdom to be closely connected with the person of Jesus, nor for an eschatology focusing on God's kingdom to lead to some form of christology. Given the centrality of Jesus' words and actions, an eschatology of the kingdom may even have called forth the christology — certainly in the case of Jesus' followers, perhaps also in the case of Jesus himself. The origin of the designation "anointed one/Messiah" for Jesus is very difficult to trace. However, on the basis of the analogy in *Psalms of Solomon* 17 we may not exclude the possibility that it was the belief in the inauguration of the kingdom of God in Jesus' mission that led to the conviction that he was a wise and perfectly obedient anointed one from the seed of

David, led by the Spirit. This conviction may have originated very early, perhaps even in Jesus' own mind.[10]

Finally one other aspect of the expectation in the *Psalms of Solomon* may be stressed. The author(s) of psalm 17 expect(s) that God will intervene quickly:

> May God hasten[11] upon Israel his mercy,
> He will deliver us from the uncleanness of unholy enemies. (v. 45)

The sins of the sinners and the persecution of God's faithful are described at length; unrighteousness prevails (vv. 5-20). For one who believes in God, and is convinced that God alone is king forever, it is evident that God cannot postpone his intervention any longer. Here, and elsewhere in similar Jewish texts, the expectation is one of the imminent reversal of fortune. In the evils of the present time, the faithful detect God's chastising and punishing hand. God is already exercising judgment, and therefore one may expect a definitive turn in the fate of the pious in Israel. In the decisive events that determine their lives negatively, God's servants put their trust in an imminent positive intervention of God. This fervent expectation enables the pious to persevere in being faithful to God's will in adverse circumstances. Future and present are inextricably linked. Contrary to the sayings of Jesus, however, the *Psalms of Solomon* reserve God's acts of mercy for the future; in the present, only his judgments are in evidence.

The Assumption of Moses

We now turn to the *Assumption of Moses*,[12] a writing commonly dated to the beginning of the first century c.e.[13] Here we find a variant in the

---

10. See further Chapter 8 below.

11. There is a variant reading *(tachynēi)* that may be explained as a future: "God will hasten." There is no contradiction with "at the time you have (fore)seen" in v. 21, just as there is no contradiction between Mark 13:30 and 13:32.

12. During the preparation of this section, I benefited much from discussions with J. Tromp. See his article "Taxo, the Messenger of the Lord," *JSJ* 21 (1990) 200-209 and particularly his *The Assumption of Moses: A Critical Edition with Commentary* (SVTP 10; Leiden: Brill, 1993). The translations below have been taken from this work.

13. I do not think we can distinguish two redactions, one to be dated in the time

eschatological scenario that sheds an interesting light on the mission of Jesus as viewed in the earliest strands of the Christian tradition. We shall focus our attention on chapters 9 and 10.

The central figure in chapter 9 is a man from the tribe of Levi called Taxo (a name that has still not been satisfactorily explained), who with his seven sons is representative of the pious in Israel for whom Moses' words in this writing are intended. He makes his appearance at a time when the ruthless "king of the kings of the earth" (8:1), who executes God's revenge and displays God's anger, rages against Israel as its last and final enemy, after the "king from the East" in 3:1 and the "mighty king of the West" in 6:8. This last mighty king, "a power with great might" (again 8:1), tortures and persecutes the faithful, trying to force them to transgress the commandments. Circumcision is forbidden, and idolatry and blasphemy are enforced, even in the temple.

In his speech in 9:2-7, Taxo views these horrible events as "a second, cruel, and unclean retribution (that) is made against the people, and a punishment without mercy, and it surpasses the first one" (v. 2). Israel has suffered much more than impious Gentiles ever had to suffer. "For what nation, or what land, or what people rebellious against the Lord, having committed many crimes, has suffered woes as great as have come over us?" (v. 3). Never have Taxo and his sons, nor their parents, nor their forefathers transgressed the commandments of the Lord. Here lies their strength. Hence Taxo suggests that, after a fast of three days, he and his sons take refuge in a cave. "Let us die rather than transgress the commandments of the Lord of lords, the God of our fathers," he says, and he continues, "For as we shall do this and die, our blood will be avenged before the Lord" (vv. 6-7).

Taxo's speech, reminiscent of the "testament of Mattathias" in 1 Macc. 2:49-70, views Israel's calamities as a severe punishment by God, a punishment far exceeding that meted out to any of the nations that have sinned against God. The hidden presupposition could be that this cannot go on; Israel will soon have been punished enough. After all, as the author of 2 Maccabees assures his readers in a crucial passage (6:12-17), God punishes his people to discipline, not to destroy them; it is a

---

of the persecution of Antiochus Epiphanes, one in the post-Herodian period (on this theory and its supporters, see O. Camponovo, *Königtum*, 142-75). Chapters 8–10, while abounding with references to the Maccabean period as portrayed in 1 and 2 Maccabees, describe the time of the End.

sign of kindness that he does so before the end, when the nations will undergo eternal punishment, having completed the measure of their sins. As we read in *As. Mos.* 12:12-13, "But it cannot happen that he will exterminate them and leave them entirely. For God, who sees everything beforehand in eternity will go out, and his covenant stands firm."

For the pious in Israel only one course is possible: they have to continue serving God. If they do so, and suffer a violent death, they will be avenged before the Lord.[14] Many commentators have explained Taxo's behavior as an effort to provoke God's vengeance, to make it impossible for him not to intervene, because the righteous in solidarity with their people increase the disproportion between sin and punishment.[15] This, however, involves an overinterpretation of Taxo's words that voice the assurance that the suffering righteous will be vindicated by God. We are reminded of the seven brothers martyred in 2 Maccabees 7 who declare: "We are ready to die rather than transgress the laws of our fathers" (v. 2), and act upon the conviction: "The Lord God is watching over us and in truth has compassion over us, as Moses declared in his song which bore witness against the people to their faces, when he said, 'And he will have compassion on his servants'" (v. 6; cf. Deut. 32:36).

For the author of the *Assumption of Moses* the king of kings and Taxo live at the end of time. He therefore expects the vindication of the suffering righteous to coincide with God's definitive intervention in the affairs of the world.[16] This final intervention is described in 10:1-10, of which vv. 1-2 form the introduction:

> And then his kingdom will appear in his entire creation,
> And then the devil will come to an end,
> And sadness will be carried away together with him.
> Then, the hands of the messenger,
> When he will be in heaven, will be filled,
> Who at once will revenge them against their enemies.

14. On this aspect, see D. C. Carlson, "Vengeance and Angelic Mediation in *Testament of Moses 9 and 10*," *JBL* 101 (1982) 85-95 (esp. 91-95).

15. Following J. Licht, "Taxo or the Apocalyptic Doctrine of Vengeance," *JJS* 12 (1961) 95-103.

16. Cf. Dan. 11:29-35; 12:1-3; *1 Enoch* 102–104; *2 Apoc. Bar.* 48:48-50; 52:7-16; Wis. 2:12-20 and 5:1-7; and Luke 6:22-23, par. Matt. 5:11-12; Mark 8:34–9:1 and par.; 13:13.

God's definitive intervention is described in v. 1 as the appearance of his kingdom. Enmity against God, personified by the devil, and sorrow will disappear. In the following verses the appearance of the kingdom is described as a theophany. "For the Heavenly One will arise from his royal throne,[17] and he will go out from his holy habitation with anger and wrath because of his sons," we read in v. 3, and v. 7 adds, "For the Highest God, the sole Eternal One, will rise, and he will manifest himself in order to punish the nations and to destroy all their idols." In fact, the announcement in Deut. 32:43 will become true: "He avenges the blood of his servants[18] and takes vengeance on his adversaries, and makes the expiation for the land of his people."

Verse 2 introduces a figure who is called *nuntius*, that is "messenger." He is obviously a priest, for the expression "to fill someone's hand(s)" that is used in connection with him is a technical term for the consecration of priests.[19] He is often thought to be an angel, serving in the heavenly sanctuary and now appointed to avenge the people.[20] Recently, however, Johannes Tromp has pointed out that it would be rather strange for an angel in heaven to be consecrated priest only at that moment.[21] He makes an interesting case for identifying Taxo — a man from the tribe of Levi, as we noted earlier — as *nuntius*, exalted to heaven and consecrated priest on high, thereby vindicated by God and joining in God's vengeance on his enemies on behalf of his servants/sons.

If this is true, there is an interesting analogy between Taxo and Jesus: both are completely obedient to God and exalted and vindicated by him; both are instrumental in bringing about the final manifestation of God's sovereign rule on earth and, in fact, in his entire creation. In the case of Taxo, exaltation and the arrival of the kingdom of God seem to coincide. The earliest traditions about Jesus seem to be contradictory on this point and so require further comment.

---

17. *A sede regni sui;* cf. *parebit regnum illius* in v. 1.

18. LXX: "of his sons," a reading that, according to the apparatus in BHS, is also found in (a) Qumran manuscript(s).

19. Cf. Exod. 28:41; 29:9; Lev. 8:33; etc. See on this point particularly Carlson, "Vengeance," 93-94.

20. The word *illos* in v. 2 remains vague. It stands parallel to *filios suos* in v. 3. It may refer back to Taxo and his sons in chapter 9, but then clearly as representatives of the true Israel. Note also that the exaltation of the messenger is followed by that of Israel in vv. 8-10.

21. Tromp, "Taxo"; idem, *The Assumption of Moses.*

A detailed analysis would reveal a number of differences. For example, Jesus is clearly not a man from the tribe of Levi, and his early followers were not a priestly community, as the group behind the *Assumption of Moses* probably was. The most striking difference obviously lies in the different assessment of the position of the devil. *"Tunc zabulus finem habebit,"* says *As. Mos.* 10:1 ("then the devil will come to his end"); there is near verbal agreement with Mark 3:26 (Vulgate): *"(Satanas) non potest stare sed finem habet"* ("[Satan] cannot stand but comes to his end"). For that reason this verse from the *Assumption of Moses* is often quoted in commentaries on this verse in Mark. But there is one decisive difference: in the saying of Jesus we do not find a future but a present; in Jesus' exorcistic activity the devil has already come to an end. The definitive breakthrough has not yet been effected, but God's rule is already manifest in Jesus' actions. In the *Assumption of Moses* Taxo can only hold out in adverse circumstances: the deliverance, though near, is yet to come. Jesus, according to early Christian tradition, has already made an attack on Satan, and made a beginning with freeing people from Satan's bonds.

Josephus on Prophets in the First Century C.E.

Many scholars have looked for parallels to the sayings of Jesus that enunciate the dynamic presence of the future kingdom of God in the words and actions of Jesus, particularly Luke 11:20, par. Matt. 12:28, and have failed to find any. A good number of scholars have therefore concluded that in this respect Jesus was unique, because he differed from all his predecessors and contemporaries. Was he really?

In his *Jesus and Judaism* E. P. Sanders has devoted much attention to this matter.[22] After rightly stressing that the failure to produce parallels should lead to the sober conclusion that the notion of the dynamic presence of the future kingdom is "otherwise unattested," and that it should not give rise to a theologically motivated discussion of Jesus' unique self-consciousness, he continues:

22. E. P. Sanders, *Jesus and Judaism* (London: SCM, 1985) 123-241, especially 123-56 and 222-41.

53

We have virtually no evidence about what other first-century Jewish healers and preachers thought about the significance of their own work. We do have, of course, some information about John the Baptist, but it can hardly be thought that we know the full range of what he thought and said. Can we be sure that neither Theudas (Josephus *AJ* XX.97-9) nor the Egyptian (*AJ* XX.169-72; *BJ* II.261-3) thought that the kingdom was breaking in with him as God's viceroy? I do not think we can. In fact, it seems likely that such prophets thought that God was at work in them and would bring in his kingdom through them.[23]

Sanders's statement deserves comment. We should note that he only puts forward a hypothesis and tells us that he thinks it is a likely one. He is rightly cautious. Our main (and often only) source of information concerning popular leaders of various types in the century preceding the Jewish-Roman conflict of 66-70 C.E. is Flavius Josephus, who gives a biased account of the events leading up to that war. On the basis of his material, modern scholars have given different pictures of the figures and groups opposed to the Romans and the Jewish establishment cooperating with them. On the whole, I prefer the approach advocated by Richard A. Horsley and John S. Hanson in their *Bandits, Prophets, and Messiahs*[24] to that found in Martin Hengel's classical book on the Zealots.[25] Horsley and Hanson stress the social and economic causes of unrest and revolt and try to show that the various leaders and groups reacted differently because they were inspired by different popular Jewish traditions. Hengel gives a comprehensive and synthetic view of what he calls the Jewish freedom movement, trying to show how it was inspired by a complete trust in God and a radical zeal for his law.

However, even Horsley and Hanson have to read between

---

23. Ibid., 138; see the wider discussion on 133-41. Sanders returns to Theudas and the Egyptian prophet in various places, but nowhere (not even in his concluding remarks on 329-40) does he put the matter so directly as in the passage just quoted.

24. R. A. Horsley and J. S. Hanson, *Bandits, Prophets, and Messiahs: Popular Movements in the Time of Jesus* (2d ed.; New York: Harper and Row, 1988).

25. M. Hengel, *Die Zeloten: Untersuchungen zur jüdischen Freiheitsbewegung in der Zeit vor Herodes I bis 70 n. Chr.* (2d ed.; AGJU 1; Leiden: Brill, 1976). On the parallels and differences between Jesus and apocalyptic prophets and Zealot popular leaders, see also Hengel's *Nachfolge und Charisma: Eine exegetisch-religionsgeschichtliche Studie zu Mt. 8:21f. und Jesu Ruf in die Nachfolge* (BZNW 34; Berlin: Töpelmann, 1968).

Josephus's lines when they ask for the ultimate motives of the popular leaders under discussion, and sometimes there is room for a different opinion. It is questionable, I think, to speak of "popular messianic uprisings at the death of Herod" when referring to the exploits of Judas, son of Hizkia, Simon, and Athronges, and about "royal pretenders and messianic movements during the Jewish Revolt" in connection with Menahem, the son of Judas the Galilean, and Simon bar Giora.[26] Neither "the messiahs" in the title of Horsley and Hanson's book, nor, for obvious reasons, "the bandits" can help us to shed light on Jesus and his movement. But what about "the prophets"?

Horsley and Hanson rightly distinguish between "oracular prophets" and "the prophetic leaders of popular movements." It is to the reports on the latter that we should turn, as E. P. Sanders has,[27] but there is not much to go on. If we pass over the related stories about the Samaritan prophet leading his people up Mount Gerizim, who was killed by the troops of Pontius Pilate (*Ant.* 18.85-87), and about Jonathan the Weaver in Cyrene a few years after the end of the Jewish War (*J.W.* 7.437-42), we have only the stories about Theudas (*Ant.* 20.97-99) and the Egyptian prophet (*J.W.* 2.261-63; *Ant.* 20.169-72) plus a story about an anonymous prophet under Festus (*Ant.* 20.188).

---

26. See de Jonge, *Christology in Context: The Earliest Christian Response to Jesus* (Philadelphia: Westminster, 1988) 160-65 and my earlier article "Josephus und die Zukunftserwartungen seines Volkes," in O. Betz, K. Haacker, and M. Hengel, eds., *Josephus-Studien* (*Festschrift* for O. Michel; Göttingen: Vandenhoeck & Ruprecht, 1974) 205-19, now in my *Collected Essays*, 48-62 (see esp. 59-62).

27. The report on Judas the Galilean in *J.W.* 2.118 and *Ant.* 18.4-9, 23-25 is also interesting. Judas (according to the *Antiquities*, he was aided by the Pharisee Saddok) is called a teacher (*sophistēs*). At the time of the census by Quirinius, he reproached his fellow countrymen for paying their taxes to the Romans and thereby tolerating human masters after serving God alone (*J.W.* 2.118; cf. 2.433). Typical of the Fourth Philosophy and its leader Judas was an "unconquerable passion for freedom, since they take God as their only leader and master" (*Ant.* 18.23). In their view, the Jewish people lived directly under the rule of God, and if they would only resist the Romans, "God would eagerly join in promoting the success of their plans, especially if they did not shrink from the slaughter that might come on them" (*Ant.* 18.5). God would establish his kingdom on earth, if only they would stand firm, whether they would be successful or die as martyrs. On Judas, see Horsley and Hanson, *Bandits, Prophets, and Messiahs*, 190-99 (whose translations I have followed). These authors view the Fourth Philosophy as a group of radical believers ready to suffer violence and death. Compare Hengel, *Die Zeloten*, 79-150, who tends to emphasize the element of armed rebellion.

Josephus's general comments on these prophets (*J.W.* 2.259-60; *Ant.* 20.167-68) are important for our purpose. He calls them "impostors and deceivers" who called upon large groups of people to follow them into the desert. "For they said that they would show them unmistakable wonders and signs done in accordance to God's plan" (so in the *Antiquities*) or, in the words of the *Jewish War,* "they persuaded the multitude to act like madmen and led them out into the desert in the belief that God would give them signs of liberation."

The prophets described here were able to mobilize large groups of people. They did not aim at armed rebellion; only in the version of his story of the Egyptian prophet in the *Jewish War* does Josephus speak of plans "to overpower the Roman garrison, to set himself up as a tyrant of the people, employing those who poured in with him as his bodyguard" (*J.W.* 2.262). Military force was used against these prophets in all cases, clearly because they created much unrest and upheaval. The crowds following the prophets clearly had very little to lose and were only too ready "to participate in the divine transformation of a world gone awry into the society of justice, willed and ruled by God."[28] They expected an imminent intervention by God, which would bring liberation and "rest from troubles."[29]

The ideas and terminology used here ("the desert," "signs," "wonders and signs," "salvation," "liberation") indicate that the prophets concerned spoke of God's intervention in terms of the Exodus and Conquest. Had the Lord not heard the voice of his people and seen their toil and their oppression? Had he not brought them out of Egypt with a mighty hand and an outstretched arm, with signs and wonders, and had he not made them enter a land flowing with milk and honey (cf. Deut. 26:7-9)? It is significant that Theudas promised that at his command the river Jordan would be parted and would provide an easy passage for the multitude. We are reminded of the Exodus through the Red Sea (Exodus 14) and the parting of the waters of the Jordan by Joshua at the entrance into the promised land (Joshua 3). Did Theudas want to lead a new exodus, with God liberating his people from Roman slavery, and/or to lead them into the land of milk and honey — or was

---

28. So Horsley and Hanson, *Bandits, Prophets, and Messiahs,* 161.

29. See *Ant.* 20.188 on the prophet under Festus, "a certain impostor who had promised them salvation and rest from troubles, if they chose to follow him into the desert."

his action only a preliminary one, bringing people to the desert in order to make an entirely new start, waiting confidently on God's intervention? The Egyptian prophet claimed to be an agent of God in the same way as Joshua in the great battle of Jericho (Joshua 6), for he promised "that at his command the walls of Jerusalem would fall down" — that is, at least, what Josephus tells us in *Ant.* 20.170.

In all these cases the prophets claim to be guided by God in a special way. Their message centers around an imminent intervention by God, which would grant a new existence to the poor and distressed in Israel who accept the message of the prophet and trust God completely. What is expected to come in the near future completely determines life in the present; people give up the little they have and follow the prophet. But did Theudas, the Egyptian, or any other prophets claim that in what they said and did the kingdom of God was already breaking in? Perhaps they did — but we do not possess any information about it. All we can say is that they were convinced that a new beginning would soon be made, and that then one saving act of God would follow the other. As Paul W. Barnett has put it: "Once the 'sign' is effected the fulfilment will inexorably follow, and soon afterwards. It is suggested that these Prophets believed that if only a 'sign' of the Exodus-Conquest could be performed, then the wheels of God would be set in motion for a re-run of His Great Saving Act."[30]

It would seem, then, that we do not find a parallel to the notion of the dynamic presence of the kingdom of God in Jesus' words and actions in contemporary Jewish writings or in reports about prophetic figures in the first century C.E.

Summary

The findings in this chapter may be summarized as follows:

1. It is not difficult to find parallels for an expectation of an imminent definitive intervention of God that determines the behavior of the faithful in the present. That present was seen as the time before the end, and it was experienced as a desperate situation crying out for

---

30. P. W. Barnett, "The Jewish Sign Prophets — A.D. 40-70: Their Intentions and Origin," *NTS* 27 (1980-81) 679-96 (quotation from 688).

action on the part of God. Many believed that God was active in the present; they also believed that he was punishing Israel in order to discipline it, or they saw his hand in the death of enemies, but no one seems to have detected any sign of the presence of the coming definitive salvation/liberation.

2. A human intermediary is not an essential element in the eschatological process. But *Psalms of Solomon* 17 shows that one could focus one's expectations on an ideal anointed son of David. This psalm, like the others in the collection, is a product of a group of pious Israelites; there is no reason to think that they had an eye on a possible candidate for that office, either in or outside their circle. The prophets described by Josephus, however, played a central part in their own expectation and in that of their followers; they were believed to be playing the role of a new Moses or a new Joshua.

3. The mysterious Taxo is a borderline case. He is a leading representative, not necessarily historical, of a group of righteous suffering servants of God. He expects vindication, but not a central role in God's intervention. But, if the new interpretation of *As. Mos.* 10:2 is right, he is not only vindicated and exalted, but appointed as a priestly messenger instrumental in God's vengeance upon his enemies and in the realization of God's sovereign rule on earth.

The picture of Taxo given by the *Assumption of Moses* helps us to understand some essential elements in early Christian, if not Jesus' own, views on Jesus' death, his resurrection/exaltation, and the final manifestation of God's kingdom. The exact relationship between personal exaltation and the final manifestation of the kingdom in Jesus' preaching requires further study in the following chapters.

4. We have found no parallels to the notion of a dynamic presence of the future kingdom in the words and actions of Jesus. We should not attach too much weight to this fact. The application of what is commonly called "the criterion of dissimilarity" in the search for the "historical Jesus" is beset with difficulties. The very moment something similar crops up from an unexpected quarter, our conclusions are no longer tenable. Let us therefore keep to the phrase "still unattested elsewhere" and not apply the categories "typical" or "unique." The search must go on.

CHAPTER 5

Jesus' Role in the Future Kingdom: Mark 14:25

Among the words on the kingdom of God attributed to Jesus in Mark and Q, the saying "Truly I tell you, I will never again drink of the fruit of the vine until that day when I drink it new in the kingdom of God" in Mark 14:25 has drawn the attention of many. It is one of the few sayings that speak about Jesus' presence at the future manifestation of God's sovereign rule in his creation and that, at the same time, hints at his death.[1] The part to be played by Jesus is, however, very modest, and the saying does not specify how Jesus, after his death, will be able to participate in the eschatological meal. Because of this lack of specifics, Mark 14:25 is thought to be early, perhaps even to go back to Jesus himself. John P. Meier speaks for many when, applying the criterion of dissimilarity, he writes: "Mark 14:25 reflects christological, soteriological, and eschatological ideas — or the startling lack thereof — that are at variance with almost any stream of early Christian tradition but are perfectly understandable in the mouth of the historical Jesus."[2] Joachim Jeremias[3] and others have pointed to the many Semiticizing and "bib-

---

1. See the brief reference to this passage on p. 38 above.

2. J. P. Meier, *A Marginal Jew: Rethinking the Historical Jesus,* vol. 2 (New York: Doubleday, 1994) 305. See also H. Patsch, *Abendmahl und historischer Jesus* (Stuttgart: Calwer, 1972) 142: "Die Authentizität des eschatologischen Wortes Jesu wird kaum je bestritten. . . . Das Wort muß für die Erforschung der eschatologischen Erwartung Jesu als fundamental angesehen werden."

3. See, e.g., J. Jeremias, *Die Abendmahlsworte Jesu* (4th ed.; Göttingen: Vandenhoeck & Ruprecht, 1967) 174-77.

lical" expressions in this verse and taken them as indication that the saying is early and perhaps even an authentic saying of Jesus.[4]

The purpose of this chapter is to take a closer look at this saying and to determine its contribution to our knowledge of the earliest Christian eschatology and christology and, if possible, also of Jesus' own expectations concerning his participation in the joy of the future kingdom of God. I shall concentrate on Mark 14:25 as such, with the parallels in Matt. 26:29 and Luke 22:18. We must allow for the possibility that the saying circulated independently and that its present position in the context of the Last Supper, immediately after the words connected with the cup in v. 24, "this is my blood of the covenant, which is poured for many," is secondary. Of course, v. 25 presupposes a meal with bread and wine that Jesus shared with his disciples at the end of his mission. It reflects a farewell situation in which Jesus speaks about the future meal in the kingdom of God, probably in the light of his impending death. This verse does not necessarily presuppose a supper as described by the Synoptics (and Paul in 1 Corinthians 11) at which Jesus instituted a solemn celebration with bread and wine by his followers after his death.[5]

The Parallels in Matthew and Luke

Matthew 26:29 closely resembles Mark 14:25 but tries to remove a number of difficulties. It avoids an awkward negation in Mark and reads "*this* fruit of the vine" (establishing a link with the preceding verse). Matthew also makes Jesus specify that he will drink the wine anew "with you" (i.e., with his disciples) and indicate his special position at the banquet as Son of the Father (replacing "in the kingdom of God" with "my Father's kingdom"). With these two changes Matthew answers two questions naturally asked by readers of Mark: Who else will be present

---

4. For further details, see M. de Jonge, "Mark 14:25 among Jesus' Words about the Kingdom of God," in W. L. Petersen, J. S. Vos, and H. J. de Jonge, eds., *Sayings of Jesus, Canonical and Non-Canonical: Essays in Honour of Tjitze Baarda* (NovTSup 89; Leiden: Brill, 1997) 123-35.

5. So I shall pass over many questions (in themselves interesting) raised by scholars in connection with Mark 14:22-25 and par., for instance, the nature of the Last Supper, the original form of the words connected with bread and wine, and the origin and nature of the liturgical meal (or meals) in the communities of Jesus' followers.

at the meal? and What will Jesus' function be? There is no doubt that Matthew is dependent on Mark in this case and therefore presents a secondary text.

But what about Luke 22:18? This verse is part of 22:15-18, which in this Gospel forms the introduction to the words about the bread and the cup in 22:19-20, parallel to Mark 14:22-24 and Matt. 26:26-28. Luke 22:18 does not follow "the words of institution" but precedes them. Moreover, it has a direct parallel in v. 16: "For I tell you, I will not eat it (= this Passover, v. 15) until it is fulfilled in the kingdom of God."

Much has been written on Luke 22:15-20 and its relationship to the other Synoptic accounts that need not detain us here.[6] The most likely theory, in my opinion, is that vv. 15-18 go back to Lukan redaction and that v. 16 was deliberately formed as a parallel to v. 18. Jacques Schlosser has argued that v. 18 is not directly dependent on Mark 14:25.[7] Because of the different endings of the saying in Mark and in Luke, he concludes that Mark and Luke give two versions, independent of one another, of a more primitive logion. He points out that the phrase "until the kingdom of God comes" cannot have been prompted by a desire on the part of the evangelist to avoid a too realistic picture of Jesus' drinking at the eschatological meal. In fact, a few verses later, in 22:30, Jesus says: "I confer on you, just as my Father has conferred on me, a kingdom, so that you may eat and drink at my table in my kingdom" (a Lukan addition to Q material; see below). Next, in 14:16-24, he gives the parable of the great supper (par. Matt. 22:1-14), introducing it with the word of a listener to earlier words of Jesus: "Blessed is anyone who will eat bread in the kingdom of God" (v. 15).

Schlosser emphasizes that the combination of "kingdom of God" and "coming" is also found in Luke 11:2, par. Matt. 6:10; Luke 17:20-21; and Mark 9:1. It is typical of words of Jesus, and so the ending of Luke may be nearer to the original logion than that of Mark. This is, however, far from certain. Luke, who had already given a reference to the kingdom of God in v. 16, may have wanted to use a different expression in v. 18,

---

6. In addition to Jeremias, *Die Abendmahlsworte Jesu,* see also H. Schürmann, *Quellenkritische Untersuchung des lukanischen Abendmahlsberichtes Lk 22, 7-38. I. Teil: Der Paschamahlbericht Lk 22, (7-14.) 15-18* (NTAbh 19/5; Münster: Aschendorf, 1953); and H. Patsch, *Abendmahl und historischer Jesus* (Stuttgart: Katholisches Bibelwerk, 1972).

7. J. Schlosser, *Le Règne de Dieu dans les dits de Jésus,* vol. 1 (Ebib; Paris: Gabalda 1980) 380-89.

forming it as an analogy to the beginning of the Lord's Prayer.[8] Schlosser's hypothesis of double attestation of an earlier saying of Jesus remains tenuous.

One final remark under this heading: In Paul's version of the tradition concerning the last meal of Jesus with his disciples in 1 Cor. 11:23-26, we find only the words over the bread and the wine. However, in the apostle's own words in v. 26, "For as often as you eat this bread and drink this cup you proclaim the Lord's death until he comes" (cf. also the *Maranatha* in 1 Cor. 16:22), there is a reference to Jesus' parousia. The coming of the Lord is parallel to the coming of the kingdom of God in the Lukan version. Paul's words show that the connection between the account of the institution of the Eucharist and God's definitive intervention in the future was made at an early stage in the tradition.

What Is Made Clear in Mark 14:25 — and What Is Left Open

Mark 14:25 has to be taken as a unity. The hypothesis that the saying once ended with "until that day," referring to the day of judgment, and that the rest of the verse is a later addition, emphasizing the duration of the time of salvation, is superfluous;[9] the use of *ekeinos* ("that") here does not call for such an interpretation.

Jesus' solemn declaration should not be taken as a vow of abstinence but as a prediction.[10] Jesus does not announce what he intends

---

8. So also Meier, *A Marginal Jew,* vol. 2, p. 367 n. 60.

9. See K. Berger, *Die Amen-Worte Jesu: Eine Untersuchung zum Problem der Legitimation in apokalyptischer Rede* (BZNW 39; Berlin: de Gruyter, 1970) 54-55; compare J. Gnilka, *Das Evangelium nach Markus (Mk 8,29–16,20)* (EKK 2/2; Zürich: Benziger Verlag; Neukirchen-Vluyn: Neukirchener Verlag, 1979) 243. Schlosser, *Le Règne de Dieu,* 386-87, is rightly critical. W. G. Kümmel, *Verheissung und Erfüllung: Untersuchungen zur eschatologischen Verkündigung Jesu* (2d ed.; Zürich: Zwingli, 1953) 29-36 (a section on "Die Rede vom eschatologischen Tag'") states: "Es ist darüber hinaus eindeutig, daß dieser kommende Gerichtstag mit dem Eintritt der Gottesherrschaft zusammenfällt (Mk 14,25)" (p. 31).

10. J. Jeremias's theory of a "Verzichterklärung Jesu" (*Die Abendmahlsworte Jesu,* 199-210) has been a hot topic in recent discussion. See also the discussion of the words "I shall not (drink) . . . until" in B. Chilton, *A Feast of Meanings: Eucharistic Theologies from Jesus through Johannine Circles* (NovTSup 72; Leiden: Brill, 1994) 38-45, 169-71. The

to do but what is going to happen "in the kingdom of God," that is, when God establishes his reign in his entire creation (cf. Luke 11:2, par. Matt. 6:9-10). He speaks authoritatively on the basis of special insight conferred by revelation.[11] John P. Meier points to the parallels in form between our verse and Mark 9:1; 13:30 ("amen + negated future action + time-span until further experience of the kingdom of God occurs"[12]). In Mark 14:25 Jesus speaks about his own future, as in the other passion predictions (see the amen sayings Mark 14:8-9, 18, 30). "Der Prophet weiß nicht nur die Geschichte, sondern auch das eng mit dem künftigen Fortgang verbundene eigene Lebensende voraus — und der Propheten-schüler (Petrus usw.) wird von seinem Meister belehrt."[13]

The eschatological nature of our logion is underscored by the use of the word *kainos* (cf. the references to the "new covenant," e.g., in Luke 22:20; 1 Cor. 11:25; 2 Cor. 3:6; Heb. 8:8; Paul's use of *a new creation* in Gal. 6:15; 2 Cor. 5:17 [with "everything old has passed away; see, everything has become new"]; and especially the saying in Mark 2:21-22 about the new wine that has to be put into fresh wineskins). The drinking of the wine will take place at a banquet to be held after God's decisive intervention in the future. Above we already mentioned the use of the same imagery in Luke 22:30 and 14:15, 16-24. The most interesting parallel is the Q passage Luke 13:28-29, par. Matt. 8:11-12, where (many) people will come from all corners of the earth to take part in a meal in the kingdom of God together with Abraham, Isaac, and Jacob.[14]

This last passage is particularly important for a better understand-

---

hypothesis that Jesus pronounced a Nazarite vow — see P. Lebeau, *Le vin nouveau du Royaume: Etude exégétique et patristique sur la Parole eschatologique de Jésus à la Cène* (Paris and Bruges: Desclée de Brouwer, 1966) 81-85, referring to M. Thurian and M. Barth — has recently been revived by M. Wojciechowski, "Le naziréat et la Passion (Mc 14,25a; 15,23)," *Bib* 65 (1984) 94-96.

11. On this, see Berger, *Die Amen-Worte Jesu.*

12. Meier, *A Marginal Jew,* vol. 2, 307. He also points to Matt. 10:23; Matt. 5:26, par. Luke 12:59; Matt. 23:39, par. Luke 13:35; and John 13:38 and remarks that this type of prediction "is a specific case of a more general biblical pattern in which it is prophesied that a person's death will not take place until some saving event occurs" (p. 306). As examples, he mentions Luke 2:26; John 21:23; and also *Jub.* 16:16 (p. 307).

13. So Berger, *Die Amen-Worte Jesu,* 67.

14. Cf. Isa. 25:6-10; 55:1-2; 65:13-14; *1 Enoch* 62:14; *2 Apoc. Bar.* 29:4; 1QSa 2:11-12. On the Old Testament and Jewish background of this saying, see D. Zeller, "Das Logion Mt 8,11f/Lk 13,28f und das Motiv der 'Völkerwallfahrt,'" *BZ* 15 (1971) 222-37 and 16 (1972) 84-93.

ing of Mark 14:25, because it too leaves much unsaid. In Mark 14:25 Jesus' position at the meal is not specified; in Luke 13:28-29 and par. he is not even mentioned. When Abraham, Isaac, and Jacob are portrayed as taking part in the meal, they are regarded as having risen from the dead (cf. Mark 12:18-27, par. Matt. 22:23-33; Luke 20:27-40), but this is not said explicitly. How the many other participants at the meal are able to be present and to take part is not specified. Also, our logion simply refers to Jesus' participation in the meal — presumably with others, but not even his disciples are mentioned. It presupposes the end of his mission among men but does not speak explicitly about his death, or about his exaltation or resurrection enabling him to take part in the meal. Neither text speaks about a "coming" of the kingdom (nor our text about a coming of Jesus); it will manifest itself at God's intervention.

When the meal will take place is clear, but where it is to be located is left open. It is assumed that in the new dispensation everything will be different and the meal is a metaphor for unity with God and all his faithful and for participation in the final salvation. With regard to the time and the location of the future meal in which Jesus will take part (with his disciples, according to Matthew), we find an interesting variety of interpretations in the early church, from the second century onwards (duly registered by Heinrich Vogels[15] and Paul Lebeau[16]).

Eschatology and christology are always closely connected. This explains why Mark 14:25 also leaves many things open regarding Jesus' place in God's dealings with humankind, during his activity in Galilee and Judea — and later. If his death is envisaged (which seems likely, given the farewell situation), nothing is said about the way he is to die and the reason for his death, nor about a possible causal connection between his departure and the manifestation of God's reign. We hear nothing about his resurrection, exaltation, or parousia. Jesus participates in the banquet, but does not preside over it or gain access to it for others,

15. H. Vogels, "Mk 14,25 und Parallellen," in N. Adler, ed., *Vom Wort des Lebens: Festschrift für Max Meinertz* (NTAbh; Münster: Aschendorf, 1951) 93-104.

16. Lebeau, *Le vin nouveau du Royaume.* The exegetical part of Lebeau's book is disappointing, but his survey of patristic exegesis is highly instructive. See also, on the version of the logion in Tatian's *Diatessaron*, A. Baumstark, "Zur Geschichte des Tatiantextes vor Aphrem," *OrChr* 30 (III 8) (1933) 1-12. For the text from the *Gospel of the Ebionites* in Epiphanius, *Panarion* 30.22.4-5 and the passage from the *Gospel of the Hebrews*, in Jerome, *De viris illustribus* II (and parallel texts), see A. F. J. Klijn, *Jewish-Christian Gospel Tradition* (VCSup 17; Leiden: Brill, 1992) 76-77 and 79-86, respectively.

for instance those closely connected with him. However, the fact that he expresses as his firm conviction that he will share in the final salvation is highly significant. Some people may want to terminate his preaching of the kingdom of God as well as his healings and exorcisms signifying its inauguration, by putting him to death, but the final breakthrough of God's sovereign rule cannot be halted, and Jesus, as messenger of the kingdom, will be personally vindicated.[17]

Mark 14:25 and Other Words of Jesus about the Future

From what has been said so far, it is clear that we should avoid overinterpreting Mark 14:25. We may try, however, to throw some more light on it by looking at it again in combination with Jesus' other sayings about the future, with regard to both his personal destiny and the final breakthrough of the kingdom. The question of the possible authenticity of our logion and related sayings will have to be discussed at a later stage.

In the words in the Synoptics concerning the future of the kingdom, all emphasis falls on the definitive revelation of God's sovereign rule. They do not pay attention to a role for Jesus at the final breakthrough, although in the present Jesus plays an important, indeed central, part — when he announces that the kingdom of God has drawn near (Mark 1:14-15) and even inaugurates it in his healings and exorcisms (see Luke 11:20, par. Matt. 12:28). He tells his disciples to pray for the coming of God's kingdom (Luke 11:2, par. Matt. 6:10); he urges people to believe his message and radically mend their ways (Mark 9:47). They are told to give up everything (Mark 10:17-31, par. Matt. 19:16-30; Luke 18:18-30) and to accept the kingdom of God as a child (Mark 10:13-16, par. Luke 18:15-17; cf. Matt. 19:13-15; 18:3). In this context the expression "to enter the kingdom of God" is used (Mark 9:47; 10:15, 23-25; see also Matt. 5:20; 7:21; 23:13; John 3:5), along with "to inherit eternal life/the kingdom of God" (Mark 10:17; Matt. 19:29; 25:34; James 2:5; and the Pauline texts 1 Cor. 6:9; 15:50; Gal. 5:21).

Both the sayings concerning the future and those dealing with the

17. See also Schlosser, *Le Règne de Dieu*, 394-95; Meier, *A Marginal Jew*, vol. 2, 307-9.

presence of the kingdom center around God's dynamic rule, soon to be fully realized but already manifest in Jesus' activity. Whatever "christology" there is, is theocentric.[18] It does presuppose, however, that the complete realization of God's rule will bring the vindication of the message preached by Jesus and thereby of his own person and mission. It seems likely that this is implied in Mark 14:25, too — a verse that is also in keeping with the other sayings about the future kingdom in not mentioning any special role for Jesus.

The same applies to Luke 13:28-29, par. Matt. 8:11-12, as we have seen in the previous section. The picture is different in Luke 22:28-30, which emphasizes that the Father confers a kingdom on Jesus, so that he is able to invite those who have stood by him in his trials to eat and drink at his table in his kingdom and to "sit on thrones judging the twelve tribes of Israel." Matt. 19:28 does not speak about table fellowship and connects the last part of this saying with the time "when the Son of Man is seated on the throne of his glory." These sayings may be linked with Mark 10:37, where James and John ask Jesus: "Grant us to sit, one at your right hand and one at your left, in your glory" (cf. also v. 40; Matt. 20:21 reads: "in your kingdom"). For the evangelist there is clearly a connection between this verse and 8:38–9:1, where he combines two originally unconnected sayings about the coming of the Son of Man "in the glory of his Father with the holy angels" and the coming of the kingdom of God "with power," respectively. Mark 10:37 as such, however, refers to an exaltation in glory of Jesus, not necessarily to his parousia.[19]

In the next chapter we shall show that the evangelists, as well as Paul before them, expected a coming of Jesus from heaven, as Lord or as Son of Man, in the near future. The dead would rise from their graves, the final judgment would take place, all wrongdoers would be punished and all satanic powers would be destroyed, and God's faithful would share in the bliss of the new dispensation. There is a great variety in the pictures of the eschatological drama, and none of them is complete. We cannot speak of a fixed scenario into which all predicted events would find a place one after the other. It may be said, however, that nearly all

18. See also Chapter 3 above and Chapter 10 below.
19. One may note that in Luke 22:28-30 and Matt. 19:28, too, neither the Son of Man nor the kingdom is said to come.

our earliest sources assign a central position to Jesus in the events of the future, just as in the past and the present.

How do we account, then, for Mark 14:25 and other passages about God's future rule which do not speak of Jesus' parousia and do not highlight the part to be played by him in the final eschatological drama? And can we say something more about the transition from a life on earth to a life in the kingdom of God presupposed in our logion, but not made explicit?

For an answer to the second question we may look for a moment to 1 Cor. 15:20-28, a passage in which the resurrection of Jesus and the resurrection of the faithful are connected. The latter will take place at Jesus' parousia; Jesus will destroy every ruler, every authority, and every power (the last enemy to be destroyed is death); the end comes when he hands over the kingdom to God the Father.

This passage has been the subject of a thorough investigation by Joost Holleman in his recent book *Resurrection and Parousia*.[20] 1 Corinthians 15 emphasizes Jesus' central role in the eschatological events and establishes a direct link between the resurrection of "those who belong to Christ" and that of Jesus Christ himself. Holleman has shown, however, that traditio-historically we should distinguish two types of resurrection: a collective resurrection at the end of times, and a personal resurrection of certain believers, immediately after their violent death.[21] Jesus' resurrection is essentially that of a martyr vindicated by God, of the type promised to the seven sons and their mother in 2 Maccabees 7. Vindication of a martyr, who has to die because he remains loyal to God and his commandments, may be to the benefit of Israel in distress, but it does not, of course, in itself bring about *final* salvation. But because Jesus was seen by his followers as one who had announced and inaugurated God's decisive and definitive intervention in human history, his vindication came to be regarded as the prelude to and the beginning of the eschatological resurrection — by Paul and perhaps also by other early Christians (but none of them has left us anything in writing).[22]

---

20. J. Holleman, *Resurrection and Parousia: A Traditio-Historical Study of Paul's Eschatology in 1 Corinthians 15* (NovTSup 84; Leiden: Brill, 1996).

21. See p. 10, n. 13 above.

22. See Holleman, *Resurrection and Parousia*, 158-61, and the publications of H. J. de Jonge mentioned above in n. 11 in Chapter 1.

For our interpretation of Mark 14:25, this may imply that Jesus' death is seen as followed by his resurrection — a resurrection envisaged as the vindication of the one who announced and inaugurated God's kingdom, and who remained faithful to his mission to the end. In his exalted state he takes part in the eschatological meal, sharing in the bliss of God's kingdom. But what, then, is the relation in time between Jesus' exaltation and the manifestation of the kingdom? 1 Cor. 15:20-28 presupposes an interim period between Jesus' resurrection and his parousia, although Paul expects it to be short.[23] In Mark 14:25 the words "never again . . . until that day" also suggest some lapse of time between Jesus' death and the meal in God's kingdom; there is, in any case, no indication that Jesus' exaltation and the appearance of God's kingdom will coincide. It is only in connection with vv. 22-24 that v. 25 suggests an interim period *of some length* during which the disciples should continue their communion with Jesus through bread and wine at a community meal.[24] Taken on its own, Mark 14:25 says no more than that Jesus expected to be resurrected/exalted and to be present at the eschatological meal at the final breakthrough of God's sovereign rule; it does not refer to Jesus' parousia and it does not give any further specifications concerning a period of "waiting" in between.

Jesus' Vindication and Exaltation

It remains remarkable, then, that our logion presupposes Jesus' vindication after his death and his participation in the joy of the future kingdom without mentioning his parousia or assigning to him a central role in the final breakthrough of God's sovereign rule. Given the importance of the notion of Jesus' parousia in early Christianity and the fact that it is found in the letters of Paul (from his oldest letter, 1 Thessalonians of about 50 C.E., onwards), as well as in Mark and in Q (followed by Matthew and Luke), those passages that fail to mention it stand out.

Do we have to explain this in terms of the diversity of eschatological expectations held by the early Christians and by Jesus himself?

---

23. In 1 Corinthians see 7:26, 29; 10:11 (". . . us, on whom the ends of the ages have come").

24. See especially Schlosser, *Le Règne de Dieu,* 394-98.

Or should we rather think in terms of development? In the latter case we may explain this difference as a sign of discontinuity in the Christian tradition, which tended to stress Christ's power and glory and to develop its christology. The texts about God's future royal rule that do not highlight Jesus' part in it would then belong to an earlier strand in the tradition than those that speak about his parousia. We shall return to this question in the two following chapters, dealing with the texts about the parousia of Jesus (Chapter 6) and the sayings about the role of Jesus as "Son of Man" in the future (Chapter 7).

We should be cautious, however, in labeling Mark 14:25 a genuine, "authentic," word of the historical Jesus. The wording of this logion does not necessarily point to a word of Jesus himself; (re)translation into Aramaic remains difficult (e.g., *kainon*, "new," as predicate). The use of *amēn legō hymin* ("Truly I tell you") is typical of Jesus in the Synoptics, and the criterion of multiple attestation as well as that of dissimilarity may be applied to it. That does not mean, however, that every individual saying of Jesus so introduced is a genuine word of Jesus; this introduction may have been added at a later stage to give it more authority. If we see what Matthew did with the word he found in Mark, and notice Luke's extensive redactional activity, we must allow for the possibility that Mark, too, dealt somewhat freely with the word handed down to him.

Again, it has become clear that we should not try to be too specific about individual sayings, but rather concentrate on historical developments. We are able to distinguish early elements in the tradition and, in some cases, to establish a link between those and the message of Jesus himself. That Jesus expected that God would vindicate his message and make him participate in the joys of the kingdom after his definitive intervention seems to me certain. After all, he must have taken his own mission seriously. Whether he expressed this conviction in the words found in Mark 14:25 remains, of necessity, uncertain.

CHAPTER 6

Jesus' Parousia

Early Christians expected Jesus to come in glory. Paul uses the Aramaic liturgical formula *Maranatha* ("Our Lord, come!") and assumes that the Corinthians know it too (1 Cor. 16:22). In his earliest letter, 1 Thessalonians, he reminds his readers of the contents of his preaching in that city with words that probably recall an early Christian creedal formula: ". . . to serve a living and true God, and to wait for his Son from heaven, whom he raised from the dead — Jesus, who rescues us from the wrath that is coming" (1 Thess. 1:9-10). The one whose coming is expected in the (near) future is Jesus, who spoke and acted on behalf of God while he wandered through Galilee with his disciples and when he went up to Jerusalem, was put to death on the cross, but was resurrected by God. This is an essential and distinctive element in early Christian expectation; at this point Jews and non-Jews who have come to put their trust in Jesus as God's final envoy differ from those Jews who do not accept Jesus.

Justin Martyr was the first to juxtapose formally Jesus' two advents, one without honor and glory and the second in glory and upon the clouds, and to adduce scriptural proof for both of them (especially Isa. 53:3 and Dan. 7:13).[1] He brings out, however, what was Christian belief

---

1. See *Dial.* 14:8; 31:1; 32:2; 34:2; 36:1; 40:4; 49:2, 7; 52:1, 4; 110:2; 120:4; 121:3 and *1 Apol.* 52:1-3. On this, see G. N. Stanton, "The Two Parousias of Christ: Justin Martyr and Matthew," in M. C. de Boer, ed., *From Jesus to John: Essays on Jesus and New Testament Christology in Honour of Marinus de Jonge* (JSNTSup 84; Sheffield: Sheffield Academic Press, 1993) 183-95.

all along. Christians and Jews expected God's final judgment and the establishment of God's sovereign rule on earth, and both used a variety of images and myths (derived from apocalyptic and other traditions about the future) to express these fundamental convictions. The Christians, however, assigned a central role to Jesus. The God who had guided Israel during the ages had decisively revealed himself in Jesus, the man from Nazareth; his words and actions had been proved right and valid by God in his resurrection, and so he was expected to act as God's intermediary at God's definitive intervention in the affairs of Israel and the entire world.

In the previous chapter we found that Mark 14:25 presupposes Jesus' vindication after his death and his participation in the joy of the future kingdom, but that it does not mention his parousia or assign to him a central role in the final breakthrough of God's kingdom on earth. It is not easy to explain this. We should keep in mind that early christology shows an extraordinary variety in conceptions; moreover, Martin Hengel has reminded us that this variety is the result of a development that took place in a remarkably short space of time.[2] We also find an interesting diversity of conceptions and expressions with regard to the notion of Jesus' participation in the final realization of God's sovereign rule, which may go back to early days. Should we, then, keep the possibility open that Jesus himself spoke about the final breakthrough of the kingdom in more than one way?[3] Or can we detect development here? We shall have to tread cautiously, both in our analysis of early Christian statements on the matter and in working back to Jesus himself.

---

2. M. Hengel, "Christology and New Testament Chronology" in *Between Jesus and Paul: Studies in the Earliest History of Christianity* (London: SCM, 1983) 30-47.

3. H. F. Bayer distinguishes between predictions of the parousia and those of the resurrection; see his *Jesus' Predictions of Vindication and Resurrection: The Provenance, Meaning, and Correlation of the Synoptic Prediction* (WUNT 2/20; Tübingen: Mohr Siebeck, 1986). See his conclusion on p. 256: "Jesus' anticipation of parousia is clearly distinguished from his anticipation of vindication and resurrection." Cf. W. G. Kümmel's treatment of the same subject in the section "Die Erwartung einer Zwischenzeit zwischen Jesu Tod und der Parusie" in his classic book *Verheissung und Erfüllung* (2d ed.; Zürich: Zwingli, 1953) 58-76. More aspects will have to be considered, however.

Paul on the Coming of Jesus

Paul and his readers expected Jesus to come in the near future. Whenever he speaks about it in his letters, Paul does not argue the fact of Jesus' coming but indicates how it will take place and how it determines (or ought to determine) the life of Christians now. In 1 Corinthians, for instance, there is the *Maranatha* in 16:22 (cf. Rev. 22:20) combined with a curse for those who do not love the Lord; a characterization of the celebration of the Lord's Supper as "proclaiming the Lord's death until he comes" (11:26); and the statement that, when the Lord comes, he "will bring to light the things now hidden in darkness and will disclose the purposes of the heart" (4:5). Jesus is called "the Lord" here, and Paul feels free to apply the expression "the day of the Lord," used in the Old Testament for the day on which God will intervene once and for all, to Jesus (see 1 Cor. 5:5; 1 Thess. 5:2; cf. similar expressions in 1 Cor. 1:8;[4] 2 Cor. 1:14; Phil. 1:6, 10; 2:16). In the four cases in 1 Thessalonians (2:19; 3:13; 4:15; 5:23) where Paul uses the term *parousia* for Jesus' coming, it is connected with the title "Lord."

When the Lord comes it will become clear who (with help from above) has persevered in love for him and who really belongs to him (see, besides 1 Cor. 4:5, also 1 Cor. 1:8; 1 Thess. 3:13; 5:23; 2 Cor. 1:14; Phil. 1:6, 10; cf. 2:16; 4:1 and 1 Thess. 2:19). The Lord will act as judge, on God's behalf (2 Cor. 5:10; cf. 1 Cor. 3:12-15; 5:5). Those who are found to be faithful "will be saved through him from the wrath of God" (Rom. 5:9; cf. 1 Thess. 1:10). In Phil. 3:20-21 we hear: "But our citizenship is in heaven, and it is from there that we are expecting a savior, the Lord Jesus Christ. He will transform the body of our humiliation that it may be conformed to the body of his glory." In 1 Thess. 4:13-18 they who are living at the time of the parousia of the Lord will be caught up in the clouds to meet the Lord in the air, together with those faithful who are raised from the dead. When in 1 Cor. 15:50-57 Paul speaks about what will happen at the last trumpet, he specifies: "the dead will be raised imperishable, and we all will be changed" (v. 52). All who are "in Christ" are destined to "be with the Lord for ever" (1 Thess. 4:17; cf. 5:10; Rom. 6:8; 2 Cor. 5:8; Phil. 1:23).

It should be noted that only in 1 Thess. 1:10; 4:16; Phil. 3:20; and

---

4. In this verse "the day of our Lord Jesus Christ" is used parallel to "the revealing *(apokalypsis)* of our Lord Jesus Christ" in v. 7 (cf. Luke 17:30).

1 Cor. 15:20-28 is Jesus' coming described in any detail; it is seen as a descent from heaven. 1 Thess. 4:16 speaks of "the archangel's call" and "the sound of God's trumpet" on the occasion (cf. Matt. 24:30-31), and 1 Thess. 3:13 of "the coming of our Lord Jesus with all his saints."

1 Cor. 15:20-28, a passage that like 1 Thess. 4:13-18 explicitly connects Jesus' parousia with the final resurrection,[5] gives a somewhat fuller scenario. At his coming those who belong to Christ will be made alive, "at the end, when he hands over the kingdom to God the Father, after he has destroyed every ruler and every authority and power" (vv. 23-24). Interestingly the word *basileia* ("kingdom") is used; Jesus rules on behalf of God until he has destroyed all opponents[6] and hands his mandate back. Verses 25-28 elaborate upon this theme in terms derived from Ps. 110:1 and Ps. 8:7 — two passages often quoted or referred to in early Christian literature (also together).[7] Other texts using Ps. 110:1 emphasize that this verse refers to a king from the family of David, who is called "Lord" (Mark 12:36 and parallels; Acts 2:34-35), but here only Jesus' appointment as *king* receives attention.[8] This kingship began when he was exalted to heaven. In Rom. 8:34 Paul, in an addition to the traditional formula concerning Jesus' death and resurrection, hints again at Ps. 110:1 when he writes: "It is Christ Jesus who died, yes was raised, who is at the right hand of God, who indeed intercedes for us." Confessing Jesus as Lord and believing that God raised him from the dead, Paul says in Rom. 10:9, will bring salvation.[9]

In 1 Cor 15:20-28, then, Jesus' parousia is connected with the full realization of the effects of his activity as king appointed by God. One should notice, however, that elsewhere in Paul's letters the parousia is

---

5. Cf. Phil. 3:20-21 and also 2 Cor. 5:1-5.

6. Cf. Phil. 3:21; 1 Pet. 3:12. No judgment is mentioned.

7. See M. de Jonge, *Christology in Context: The Earliest Christian Response to Jesus* (Philadelphia: Westminster, 1988) 186-88 and (in greater detail) M. Hengel, " 'Sit at my Right Hand!': The Enthronement of Christ at the Right Hand of God and Psalm 110:1," in *Studies in Early Christology* (Edinburgh: Clark, 1995) 119-225.

8. Ps. 8:5 uses the expression "son of man"; it does not play any role in this passage. Paul never uses it in connection with Jesus.

9. Cf. also Rom. 14:9 and the hymn in Phil. 2:6-11 with the phrase "and every tongue should confess that Jesus Christ is Lord, to the glory of God the Father." Other statements on Jesus' exaltation are found in Acts 2:32-36; 5:31; cf. also Luke 23:43; Heb. 5:9-10; 9:11-12; 12:2 (and with a particular "Johannine twist" in John 3:14; 8:28; 12:32-34).

never explicitly mentioned together with the kingdom of God.[10] He does use the latter expression a few times; so, for instance, in 1 Thess. 2:12, where he speaks of his urging and encouraging and pleading "that you lead a life worthy of God, who calls you into his own kingdom and glory." The arrival of this kingdom no doubt coincides with Jesus' parousia mentioned five times in the same letter (see above), but the two events are never explicitly linked. In two passages (1 Cor. 6:9-10 and Gal. 5:19-21) Paul warns his readers that the unrighteous will not inherit the kingdom of God, and he gives specifications of wrong behavior. In 1 Cor. 15:50 (cf. 51-57) he emphasizes that "flesh and blood cannot inherit the kingdom of God." The phrase "inherit the kingdom of God" is also found in other writings (Mark 10:17; Matt. 19:29; 25:34; James 2:5) and may be regarded as traditional. In the four passages just mentioned and in 1 Cor. 15:20-28, the future breakthrough of the kingdom is in view,[11] together with the preparation of the believers for it, as well as their participation in it. Paul, no doubt, ascribes to Jesus a role in this kingdom, but only in 1 Cor. 15:23-28 does he say so in so many words, very probably connecting originally different lines of thought.

One further remark should be made. In 1 Cor. 15:23-28 Jesus' appointment as king is thought to have taken place when he was exalted to heaven at his resurrection. In v. 23 two resurrections are mentioned: "But each in his own order: Christ the firstfruits, then at his coming those who belong to Christ." Here a direct relationship is established between the resurrection of Jesus and that of those who are "of/in Christ" (see also 1 Thess. 4:14; 1 Cor. 6:14; Rom. 6:5, 8; 8:11; and cf. Rom. 8:17; Phil. 3:21; 1 Cor. 15:51-52). Yet we should be aware that this connection between the resurrection of Jesus Christ on the one hand and that of those belonging to him at the parousia on the other is secondary. Creedal formulas concerned with Jesus' resurrection, his death, and his death and resurrection together, play a significant part in early Christianity, as Paul's letters show,[12] but in none of them are his resurrection and his coming in the future connected.[13] As Henk Jan

10. On this, see above, Chapter 3, pp. 35-36.

11. In 1 Cor. 4:20 and Rom. 14:17 Paul emphasizes the dynamic presence of the kingdom in the life of the community.

12. See my *Christology in Context*, 36-39.

13. In 1 Thess. 1:9b-10, however, the phrase "whom he raised from the dead" is part of a larger, probably equally traditional and certainly not specifically Pauline formula that also speaks of the parousia of the Son of the living, true God.

de Jonge and Joost Holleman have demonstrated in detail, Jesus' resurrection is essentially that of a martyr vindicated by God, in the manner found in 2 Maccabees 7.[14] It acquired eschatological significance because Jesus was regarded by his followers (even before his death) as God's eschatological agent. Vindication of a martyr, put to death because of his loyalty to God and his commandments, does not necessarily bring about final salvation; but because Jesus died as the agent of God's decisive and definitive intervention in human history, his vindication came to be regarded as the beginning of the eschatological resurrection.

Jesus' Coming in the Synoptic Gospels

In the first three Gospels we find a variety of statements about Jesus' coming. In this section we will give special attention to Q and Mark, but time and again we shall have to point to further developments in Matthew and Luke. Again we will ask whether and how this coming is linked to the arrival of the kingdom. We will also investigate the connection between Jesus' resurrection and his parousia. A new element is the use of the term "Son of Man" for Jesus in sayings attributed to Jesus himself.

In Q there is first of all Luke 12:39-40, par. Matt. 24:43-44 — one of the many sayings about watchfulness: "But know this: if the owner of the house had known at what hour the thief was coming, he would not have let his house be broken into.[15] You also must be ready, for the Son of Man is coming at an unexpected hour." This saying is followed by one about a faithful and prudent manager (Luke 12:42-46, par. Matt. 24:45-51) who performs his duties in accordance with his master's instructions. "Blessed is that slave whom his master *(kyrios)* will find at work when he arrives" (Luke 12:43, par. Matt. 24:47; contrast v. 46 and vv. 50-51 respectively). A parallel is found in Mark 13:33-37, which uses the image of the doorkeeper who is ordered to watch. "Therefore, keep awake, for you do not know when the master of the house will come

14. See pp. 7-10, 67 above.
15. The simile of the thief is used in connection with "the day (of the Lord)" in 1 Thess. 5:2, 4 (cf. 2 Pet. 3:10) and in Rev. 3:3; 16:15 in connection with the coming of Jesus himself.

(cf. Matt. 24:42) . . . or else he may find you asleep when he comes suddenly." The same theme is elaborated upon in the parable of the ten virgins (Matt. 25:1-13, with its counterparts in the passages in Luke 12:35-38 and 13:25-27) and the twin parables of the talents and of the pounds (Matt. 25:14-30 and Luke 19:11-27).

Related is the admonition in Mark 13:28-29, par. Matt. 24:32-33; Luke 21:29-31, immediately following some verses describing the coming of the Son of Man. Using the image of the fig tree that puts forth its leaves when the summer draws near, the saying warns: "So also when you see these things taking place, you know that he (or: it) is near, at the very gates." Luke explains: "you know that the kingdom of God is near." A little later the same Gospel has another admonition to be on guard, because "that day" comes unexpectedly (Luke 21:34-38). "Be alert at all times, praying that you may have the strength to escape all these things that will take place, and to stand before the Son of Man" (v. 36). At another place the central question is: "When the Son of Man comes, will he find faith on earth?" (Luke 18:8).

The day of Jesus' coming will be one of judgment. Those who have put their trust in him and have accepted the duties connected with a life in his service will have to give an account of what they have done in the time between his departure and his return (although the latter word is not used). Jesus is the Lord who demands an account of his servants; he is also called Son of Man. The situation presupposed here is clearly one of communities of believers waiting for the parousia, which (at least theoretically) may come any moment, but is as yet outstanding.

Another Q logion has to be mentioned in this connection, Luke 13:34-35, par. Matt. 23:37-39. Again the word "return" is avoided, yet Jesus' mission now is connected with his future coming: "Jerusalem, Jerusalem, the city that kills the prophets and stones those who are sent to it! How often have I desired to gather your children together as a hen gathers her brood under her wings, and you were not willing. See your house is left to you (Matthew adds "desolate"). And I tell you, you will not see me until the time comes when you say: 'Blessed is he who comes in the name of the Lord.'"[16]

16. The expression "blessed is the one who comes in the name of the Lord," taken from Ps 118:26, is also used in Mark 11:9, par. Matt 21:9; Luke 19:38, by those who cheer Jesus at his entry in Jerusalem.

For a description of the nature of Jesus' coming, we have to turn to a number of Son of Man texts. Here Mark is more outspoken than Q, because he uses the image found in Dan. 7:13 of "one like a son of man coming with the clouds of heaven" to denote a movement by Jesus as the Son of Man from heaven to earth (see Mark 13:26-27, par. Matt. 24:30-31; Luke 21:27; Mark 14:62, par. Matt. 26:64; also Mark 8:38, par. Matt. 16:27, 28; Luke 9:26). In Mark 8:38 and 13:27, par. Matt. 24:31 he is accompanied by angels. They are sent out to gather his elect from the four winds (Mark 13:27, par. Matt. 24:31). The overall picture is rather similar to that in 1 Thess. 4:13-18, only there the term "Son of Man" is not used.[17]

Q is considerably less explicit in a number of connected statements in Luke 17:24, 26, 30, par. Matt. 24:27, 37, 39. Matthew speaks consistently about "the *parousia* of the Son of Man" (see also 24:3) and is clearly secondary; one may compare the Pauline instances of *parousia* mentioned in the previous section. Luke speaks about the day(s) of the Son of Man (also in 17:22). The word "coming" is not used; v. 24 compares the Son of Man in his day with a flash of lightning that "lights up the sky from one side to another," and v. 30 speaks of "the day on which the Son of Man is revealed" (cf. 1 Cor. 1:7). Just as in Mark 13:24-27, par. Matt. 24:29-31; Luke 21:25-28 the coming of the Son of Man is accompanied with a cosmic upheaval, so in Luke 17:26-27, par. Matt. 24:37-39 the accompanying circumstances are compared to the Flood (Luke 17:28-29 adds the example of the fire and sulfur that rained from heaven and destroyed all people in Sodom). Finally, we should note the differences between Q and Mark in the case of the saying preserved in Mark 8:38. Mark pictures the Son of Man coming in glory with his holy angels; he will be ashamed of all who are ashamed of Jesus and his words now. Luke 12:8-9, par. Matt. 10:32-33 does not mention a coming of the Son of Man to earth, but only a (heavenly?) court in which the Son of Man acknowledges before the angels of God everyone who acknowledges him before others (cf. Acts 7:55-56).

As far as Mark and Q are concerned, Mark 8:38–9:1 is the only passage that explicitly links the coming of the Son of Man with the arrival of the kingdom of God.[18] This connection is undoubtedly redactional; the text also speaks of a coming "in power" just as Mark 13:26

---

17. Matt. 24:31 mentions "a loud trumpet call"; cf. 1 Thess. 4:16; 1 Cor. 15:52.
18. See p. 38 above.

describes the coming of the Son of Man with the clouds "with great power and glory." This connection, exceptional and secondary in Mark (as in the letters of Paul), is, however, found more often in Luke and Matthew.

In Luke we already noticed the statement "the kingdom of God is near" in 21:31 following the text about the coming of the Son of Man in 21:27.[19] Remarkably, the texts about the day(s) of the Son of Man in 17:22-30 follow a discussion between the Pharisees and Jesus about the kingdom of God, leading to the statement "the kingdom of God is among you" (17:20-21). This emphasis on the present manifestation of God's sovereign rule in the words and actions of Jesus makes the evangelist continue with a reference to the final breakthrough of that rule. In Luke 19:11 the parable of the pounds is introduced with the statement that Jesus told it "because they supposed that the kingdom of God was to appear immediately." In that parable (19:12-27) the central person is a nobleman who goes to a distant country to get royal power for himself. When he returns (here the expression "return" occurs; two different Greek words are used, in v. 12 and in v. 15), having received royal power (v. 15), he summons his servants to render account and punishes those who did not want him to become king over them. A similar picture is found when we combine 22:69 — "From now on the Son of Man will be seated at the right hand of the power of God" (cf. Ps. 110:1; a coming on the clouds of heaven, as in Mark 14:62; Matt. 26:64, is omitted) — with 23:42, "Jesus, remember me when you come into your kingdom" (equated with "paradise" in the next verse; cf. also 24:26, and 1:32-33). These two texts may be connected, again, with Acts 1:3, 6, which reports discussions between Jesus and his disciples about the kingdom of God ("is this the time you will restore the kingdom to Israel?" v. 6) and 1:11, where angels announce: "This Jesus, who has been taken up from you into heaven, will come in the way you saw him go into heaven."

In Matthew three passages deserve our attention.[20] First it should be noted that Matt. 16:27-28 introduces the Son of Man also in the second clause and speaks about "the Son of Man coming in his king-

---

19. Luke 9:26-27, like Mark, combines the coming of the Son of Man and the appearance of the kingdom (but omits the words "having come with power").

20. I mention Matt. 10:23, "you will not have gone through all the towns of Israel before the Son of man comes," only for the sake of completeness. On Matt. 19:28, see p. 38 and p. 66.

dom." The same is found in the explanation of the parable of the tares in 13:36-43, which has the statement "The Son of Man will send his angels, and they will collect out of his kingdom all causes of sin and evildoers" (v. 41).[21] We may also point to the rule of the Son of Man as judge and king in 25:31-46, a story illustrating the activities mentioned in 16:27-28. As king, the Son of Man is in a position to declare: "Come, you that are blessed by my Father, inherit the kingdom prepared for you from the foundation of the world" (v. 34).

Are there any passages where Jesus' coming is related to his resurrection? Central to our inquiry are the three predictions by Jesus of his passion and resurrection in Mark 8:31; 9:31; 10:33-34.[22] They betray knowledge of the events that would take place later on and are clearly redactional; they were taken over by Matthew and Luke (Matt. 16:21; 17:22-23; 20:18-19 and Luke 9:22, 44; 18:32-33). It is often argued that these three passages are developments of a shorter, earlier creedal statement about Jesus' death and resurrection (something like 9:31). In any case, in their basic form these three statements resemble other double formulas concerning Jesus' death and resurrection, particularly the "contrast formulas" found in Acts 2:22-24, 36; 3:13; 4:10; 5:30; 10:39-40; and 13:28-30.[23] In Acts the emphasis is on the hostility of those who caused Jesus' death and on God's vindication of Jesus by raising him from the dead. The latter idea is expressed differently by Mark, but no doubt he also wants to emphasize that Jesus was raised by God.[24]

At the end of Mark these predictions are taken up by the declaration of the young man in the empty tomb that Jesus of Nazareth who was crucified has been raised (Mark 16:6, par. Matt. 28:5-6). This is followed by a command to the disciples and Peter to follow Jesus to Galilee (Mark 16:7, par. Matt. 28:7; cf. Mark 14:28, par. Matt. 26:32). The use of the verb "to see" reminds one of the statements concerning Jesus' parousia in Mark 13:26 and 14:62, and of the prediction in 9:1: "some standing here . . . will not taste death until they see that the

---

21. Note the Matthean expression "the sons of the kingdom" in v. 38 (and 8:12) and the statement "the righteous will shine like the sun in the kingdom of their Father" in v. 43.

22. In what has been preserved of Q, nothing is said about Jesus' death and resurrection.

23. See de Jonge, *Christology in Context*, 108-9.

24. Mark has "after three days he will rise again," changed by Matthew to "on the third day he will be raised" (see also Luke 9:22; 13:32; 18:33; 24:7, 42; Acts 10:40) — a more familiar and a more traditional phrase (see 1 Cor. 15:3-5).

kingdom of God has come in power." Some scholars have found an announcement of Jesus' parousia in Galilee in Mark 16:7,[25] but it seems more likely that the evangelist, like the tradition before and after him, meant an appearance of the risen Jesus, confirming his vindication and exaltation as well as commissioning the disciples to bring the gospel to all people. That is, at least, the way Matthew (who has the risen Jesus repeat the command to go to Galilee in 28:10) pictured it. In Matt. 28:16-20 the risen Jesus assures his disciples in Galilee that all authority in heaven and earth has been given to him and that he will be with them to the end of the age; at the same time, he orders them to go out into the world. This fits in with the fact that in Jesus' reply to the high priest in Matt. 26:64 the coming of the Son of Man on the clouds is preceded by his being seated "at the right hand of the Power" (cf. Ps. 110:1). Mark too has "you will see the Son of Man seated at the right hand of the Power" in 14:62; he therefore knows of Jesus' exaltation, although he does not explicitly connect it with his resurrection[26] and does not emphasize it as much as Matthew and Luke.[27]

As to the vindication of the disciples, we note that Mark not only warns them to be watchful (see above) but also promises "that he who endures to the end will be saved" (13:13, concluding a passage on persecution and tribulation). When the Son of Man comes, his angels will be sent out to collect his elect from all corners of the earth (13:27). Immediately following on 8:31, the crowd and the disciples hear that "those who lose their life for my sake, and for the sake of the gospel, will save it" (8:35). In fact, they will meet the Son of Man coming in the glory of his Father with his holy angels (8:38), and some of those listening now to Jesus will see that the kingdom of God has come with power (9:1).[28]

It strikes us that in the case of the disciples the emphasis is on the blessings of God's kingdom at its final breakthrough in power, and not

---

25. See, e.g., the discussion in R. Pesch, *Das Markusevangelium*, vol. 2 (HTKNT 2/2: Freiburg: Herder, 1977) 525-28, 534-35, 538-41.

26. See also the story of Jesus' transfiguration in 9:2-8, 9-13 shortly after 8:31.

27. See the discussion of Luke 19:12-27 and 22:69 (the parallel of Mark 14:62) together with related texts, and of Matt 16:27-28; 13:36-43; and 25:31-46 above pp. 78-79 — and also the remarks on Jesus' exaltation in connection with 1 Cor. 15:20-28 (above, pp. 74-75).

28. Note the "some"; clearly a considerable period of time has elapsed between the time of Jesus and the moment this was written (cf. also 13:28-37, especially v. 30).

on their individual resurrection. The same is true of Q, in which Jesus' teaching in all probability began with the four beatitudes recorded in Luke 6:20-23. Those who are poor will receive a share in the kingdom of God, those who are hungry now will be satisfied, and those who weep now will laugh (vv. 20-21). So also those who suffer hardship on account of the Son of Man may know that their reward is great in heaven (vv. 22-23).

This is not the place to go into details, but a few remarks may be helpful.[29] The beatitude in Luke 6:22-23 links up with a number of early statements in which Jesus is portrayed as the final envoy of God in a long series of prophets sent by God and rejected by (the leading figures in) Israel; his disciples share in his fate. In this early model of interpretation of Jesus' death, his mission is vindicated in the final judgment that is soon to come, which will bring punishment for all those who disobeyed him as envoy of God — and, according to Luke 6:22-23, a reward for those who remained faithful to him.

The other sayings on discipleship are reminiscent of Old Testament and early Jewish sayings of God's vindication of those who, in distress and oppression, continue to place their trust in God. Jesus was also portrayed by early Christians as a suffering righteous servant of God, for instance in the different versions of the passion narrative. In the various passages on God's help for his suffering servants, the vindication may take different forms, and it is often not so easy to trace how the author in question envisages it.[30] It would seem that vindication was the central notion. It could either be expressed in terms of the antithesis between death and resurrection, or presented in terms of God's final triumph, the realization of God's kingdom in power. In this respect we may also point to Paul, who at one stage expected to be among the living at the parousia and to belong to those who would be "changed" in order to be with the Lord for ever (1 Thess. 4:14-17; 1 Cor. 15:50-57). Later, during his imprisonment in Philippi, however, he expected to die before this event. He then speaks of his "desire . . . to depart and be with Christ" (Phil. 1:23) and of knowing "Christ and the power of his resurrection and the sharing of his sufferings by becoming

29. See also above, pp. 15-22.

30. See also Chapter 9b in J. Holleman, *Resurrection and Parousia: A Traditio-Historical Study of Paul's Eschatology in 1 Corinthians 15* (NovTSup 84; Leiden: Brill, 1996), with (among other things) an analysis of Wisdom of Solomon 2–4.

like him in his death, if somehow I may attain the resurrection from the dead" (3:10-11). In the same letter he continues to refer to what will take place at Jesus' coming, using the first person plural (3:20-21).

Early Christian Statements on the Nature of Jesus' Coming

Neither the statements on Jesus' coming in Paul's letters nor those in Q and Mark (with Matthew and Luke) aim at giving a precise description of a particular component of a fixed scenario. Jesus' coming, like other events expected to take place in the future, is only mentioned when there is reason to do so, and a complete picture of all that will happen at the turn of the times is presented nowhere. All statements are made in the context of admonition, encouragement, and consolation of the communities of followers of Jesus for which the authors wrote. Hence the emphasis on watchfulness, on being prepared to render account, on leading a life worthy of God, and on being blameless on the day of the Lord/Son of Man. That day will bring judgment and separation between those who have been faithful and those who have not. Those who belong to Jesus will be saved, either by being transformed or by being raised to a new life.

Only a few times is the coming of Jesus described as a coming from heaven. Mark introduces here the imagery of Dan. 7:13. Mark and Q, followed by Matthew and Luke, often use the term "Son of Man" (over against Paul, who prefers "the Lord"). *Parousia* is found four times in Paul and in Matthew each, but it is not used consistently as a more or less technical term. Jesus plays a central role in the future events; that much is clear, but why and how he received this role is usually not spelled out. His vindication by God in his resurrection is an event that receives a central place in early Christian creedal formulae (and later). Because Jesus was raised as a person through whom God had spoken and acted decisively, his resurrection was seen as the exaltation of a king chosen by God who could be called "Lord" and who would soon destroy all opposition to God's rule. But only seldom are Jesus' resurrection, exaltation, and future coming expressly related. The same applies to the connection between his coming and the arrival of God's kingdom "in power" (to use Mark's expression again).

Our earliest written Christian sources, then, though not presenting a fixed scenario, presuppose a picture of past, present, and future events in which a central position is assigned to Jesus. The picture is composed of a number of elements that represent different and originally unconnected traditions.

How is this to be reconciled with our findings in Chapter 5? It remains very remarkable that the sayings dealing with God's kingdom in the future do not mention a role for Jesus at the final breakthrough; all emphasis is on the final realization of *God's* sovereign rule. At the same time, Jesus' role in the present is very important, indeed central. It is he who announces that the kingdom is at hand, who inaugurates it in his battle against Satan and his demons, and who challenges those who listen to him to make the right decision: to accept the good news and to adjust their lives accordingly.

Evidently, one could speak of a future manifestation of God's sovereign rule in his entire creation without highlighting in it the role assigned to Jesus — although he was the one appointed to announce the final breakthrough, to summon people to prepare themselves for it, and even to inaugurate it. All who respond positively to the good news and turn to God will have a share in the blessings of the kingdom, together with the faithful of the past, and with Jesus himself (Luke 13:28-29, par. Matt. 8:11-12; Mark 14:25).

Only in Luke 22:28-30, par. Matt. 19:28 (together with Mark 10:35-40, par. Matt. 20:20-23) does Jesus' role as ruler and judge, together with the Twelve, receive attention. Neither here nor in related passages do we hear of a coming from heaven to earth. We may point to the parallel with Luke 12:8-9, par. Matt. 10:32-33 and refer to the Q texts on the Son of Man in Luke 17:24, 26, 30, which also avoid the term "coming." The kingdom manifests itself and the judgment takes place at a certain moment in the future. The present dispensation will be superseded by a new state of affairs in which God's name will be hallowed and God's will done. This will take place in the near future, but no timetable is given; in Mark 14:25, however, the phrase "never again . . . until that day" suggests that Jesus' death and vindication and the manifestation of the kingdom will not coincide.

The material presented in this chapter shows a great variety in the expectations among early Christians concerning God's definitive intervention in the future. Once again we ask: Can we trace developments, and can we distinguish between later and early traditions? We realize, of course, that where Paul, Q, and Mark agree this multiple attestation carries us back very early in the history of the groups of Jesus' followers. However, in this case the fact that the more or less coherent picture arising from the evidence is composed of elements representing originally unconnected traditions should make us hesitate to go back even further, to the time of Jesus' mission before his death. Furthermore, the presence of a number of other passages that do not fit into the overall picture — although they are not necessarily contradictory, given the variety in early Christian christology and the complementary nature of early Christian thinking — should make us cautious.

Is it possible to go back further with the help of the criterion of dissimilarity? Again, we should proceed very carefully. It would be unwise to concentrate on individual passages; we should rather base any conclusions on more general patterns visible in the material at hand. For instance, the evidence collected above shows that, at a very early stage, Jesus' followers expected a complete change in the affairs of this world that would bring bliss for the faithful and judgment for evildoers and all powers hostile to God; they assigned a central role to Jesus, as Lord or Son of Man, in this event. It is reasonable to assume that they connected God's final intervention and Jesus' coming, because already before his death the followers of Jesus expected a final breakthrough of the kingdom of God, which he announced and inaugurated. Their experiences after his death, interpreted as appearances of the risen Jesus, vindicated by God, led to the conviction that his message concerning the complete realization of God's rule remained valid, that the final breakthrough would, therefore, take place soon, and that Jesus would have a central role in it.

What are we able to say about Jesus himself? Many scholars agree that the notion of the kingdom of God was central to Jesus' message and mission; this included the expectation of the speedy revelation of God's sovereign rule in his entire creation (see Chapter 3). Jesus would have expected to participate in this complete realization together with all who were faithful to God in the present and the past. Because of the centrality of the theme in the belief of his followers after his death on the cross, it is difficult to determine exactly how Jesus himself viewed his death, and life beyond death.[31] If, at least towards the end of his mission, he had to reckon seriously with the possibility that the hostility which he encountered would lead to his violent death, he must have

31. See above, pp. 18-22.

believed in some form of vindication by God after his death. The messenger would be vindicated together with his message.

The question is, then, whether this vindication included a "coming" (in fact, a return) with a central role in the establishment of God's kingdom. If we recall the secondary nature of the connection between Paul's and Mark's statements on the future rule of God and those on the parousia, and bear in mind that not one of the passages speaking about the future kingdom actually mentions a "coming" of Jesus in the future, we should hesitate to give a positive answer.

CHAPTER 7

The Exaltation of Jesus,
the Son of Man

In search of an answer to the question with which the previous chapter ended, we shall look again at the passages in Mark and Q on the future revelation/coming of the Son of Man — very briefly, however, in view of the vast amount of literature devoted to the problem of the Son of Man in the Gospels.

Jesus as the Son of Man

The designation Son of Man is found only in the four Gospels and once in Acts. With the exception of John 12:34 and Acts 7:56, it is always used by Jesus himself. The very unusual Greek expression represents Semitic idiom; invariably the definite article is used: "*the* Son of Man."[1] The expression is not found in Paul, let alone in the traditional material incorporated in his letters, nor in later writings of the New Testament.

1. An exception is John 5:27. The Greek expression is *ho huios tou anthrōpou,* in which the second noun has the article in accordance with New Testament Greek usage. M. Hengel has argued that this uniform rendering of an Aramaic term points to an early translation of the Jesus tradition at a particular place; see his *Between Jesus and Paul: Studies in the Earliest History of Christianity* (London: SCM, 1983) 27-28. C. F. D. Moule, *The Origin of Christology* (Cambridge: Cambridge University Press, 1977) 13, is of the opinion that the definite article was used because the term was intended to refer expressly to Daniel's "one like a son of man." See also his recent article " 'The Son of Man': Some of the Facts," *NTS* 41 (1995) 277-79.

86

Only in Rev. 1:13 and 14:14 does "one like a son of man" occur, clearly influenced by Dan. 7:13. At a later stage, in discussion with a non-Jewish audience, "Son of Man" clearly was no longer a suitable designation to explain Jesus' dignity and his relationship to God and humanity.

In the Gospels only Jesus uses this expression, and it is, I think, always in reference to himself — though this has been disputed. In Mark it is used to indicate Jesus' authority on earth. The Son of Man has authority to forgive sins (2:10), and he is Lord even over the Sabbath (2:28). The designation is used when Jesus predicts his death and resurrection (8:31; 9:9-12; 9:31; 10:33), or his death alone (14:21, 41). He uses it when he speaks about his future coming in glory (8:38; 13:26; 14:62); in the last two texts there is a clear allusion to the coming of "one like a son of man" in Dan. 7:13-14; and in 8:38–9:1 and 14:62 there is a link with the coming of the future kingdom of God. The use of this designation in Q is less explicit. There is no reference to suffering and death and no direct connection with Dan. 7:13. It is stated, however, that the Son of Man is sent by God with authority and expects people to give careful attention to his message. Some people give up everything and follow him; the people of "this generation" reject him (see Luke 7:34, par. Matt. 11:19; Luke 9:58, par. Matt. 8:20; Luke 11:30 and Matt. 12:40 [slightly different]). Those who obey him will be vindicated: "And I tell you, every one who acknowledges me before others, the Son of Man also will acknowledge before the angels of God; but he who denies me before others will be denied before the angels of God" (Luke 12:8-9, par. Matt. 10:32-33). The designation "Son of Man" is here clearly connected with the future judgment (though the Son of Man is not expected to act as judge himself). The future Son of Man is also found in Luke 12:40 (par. Matt. 24:44); 17:22, 24, 26, 30 (par. Matt. 24:27, 37, 39). These texts speak about the sudden arrival of the Son of Man; the disciples should be watchful and prepared, unlike the people of this generation, who continue their all-too-human pursuits.

We cannot vouch for the authenticity of each individual saying about the Son of Man, even in Mark and Q. But the fact that this unusual Greek expression is used — and is used exclusively in words of Jesus, whereas early Christians did not employ it in their own preaching (except when words of Jesus were concerned)[2] — makes it likely that

---

2. It continues to play an important role in the Fourth Gospel, for instance.

"Son of Man" belongs to the oldest layers of tradition, if not to Jesus' own vocabulary.

If Jesus did use the term himself, what did he mean by it? Much has been written about the possible meanings of the Aramaic expression *bar (e)nash(a)* in Jesus' time. Was it used as a circumlocution for "I" or in general statements in which the speaker could, at times, include himself, or did it denote a class of persons with whom the speaker identified himself ("a man like myself").[3] A number of Greek sayings are often considered to be the result of misunderstanding and consequent mistranslation. At the later stages of transmission of the sayings represented by Mark and Q, however, the term "Son of Man" is in any case used as an exclusive self-reference.

At the same time, the label does not unequivocally disclose the identity of the speaker. Nowhere in the Gospels do those who respond to Jesus positively declare, "You are the Son of Man!" — though they do confess him as the Messiah (so Peter, for instance, in Mark 8:29) — and nowhere do his opponents take him up on this self-designation — though in Mark 14:61 the high priest asks Jesus explicitly, "Are you the Christ, the Son of the Blessed?" Mark and Q clearly do not regard "Son of Man" as a title readily understood (and then misunderstood when used in connection with Jesus) by all.[4]

This state of affairs makes it likely that Jesus did in fact speak of himself as "the Son of Man," a designation not directly understood by outsiders, but for him and insiders referring to "the one like a son of man" in Daniel 7, understood in the way suggested by C. K. Barrett, Morna D. Hooker, and Graham N. Stanton.[5] In any case, the designation implied obscurity, homelessness and rejection, humility, service, suffer-

3. See, for instance, G. Vermes, *Jesus the Jew: A Historian's Reading of the Gospels* (2d ed.; London: Collins, 1977) 160-91; J. A. Fitzmyer, "The New Testament Title 'Son of Man' Philologically Considered," in *A Wandering Aramean: Collected Aramaic Essays* (SBLMS 25; Missoula, Mont.: Scholars Press, 1979) 143-160; M. Casey, *Son of Man: The Interpretation and Influence of Daniel 7* (London: SPCK, 1979); and B. Lindars, *Jesus, Son of Man: A Fresh Examination of the Son of Man Sayings in the Gospels in the Light of Recent Research* (London: SPCK, 1983).

4. This is brought out clearly by J. D. Kingsbury, *The Christology of Mark's Gospel* (Philadelphia: Fortress, 1983) 157-70.

5. See C. K. Barrett, *Jesus and the Gospel Tradition* (London: SPCK, 1967); M. D. Hooker, *The Son of Man in Mark* (London: SPCK, 1967); G. N. Stanton, *Jesus of Nazareth in New Testament Preaching* (SNTSMS 27; Cambridge: Cambridge University Press, 1974).

ing, and ultimately death. It also denoted authority (disputed, however, until the disclosure of Jesus' true identity) and, of course, final vindication at the full realization of God's sovereign rule on earth. We may say with some confidence that the term "Son of Man" applied by Jesus to himself had the connotation of suffering, death, and vindication of the obedient servant of God par excellence, who appeared at a crucial moment in the history of Israel and the world.[6] To what extent further details in the Son of Man sayings in Mark and Q (and elsewhere) reflect Jesus' own views escapes our knowledge.

The sayings about future activities of the Son of Man are often thought to go back to Jesus, but particularly on the basis of Luke 12:8-9, some scholars have concluded that he spoke not about himself but about someone else closely connected with him.

With many other scholars Henk Jan de Jonge is of the opinion that the use of the Semitizing expression "Son of Man" points to a very early stage in the tradition.[7] He thinks that Jesus spoke about the Son of Man as a figure appearing and acting in the (near) future, but without identifying himself with that figure. A crucial text is the Q passage in Luke 12:8-9, par. Matt. 10:32-33 (cf. Mark 8:38). Later Jesus' followers identified Jesus with the coming Son of Man; still later this identification led to the introduction of the term in sayings dealing with his authority among men, and with his death and resurrection. De Jonge adduces as an additional argument that Jesus' message centers around the breakthrough of the kingdom of God; "for the preaching of the kingdom, the identity of the Son of Man was irrelevant," he says, "and the identification of the Son of Man with Jesus, superfluous."

Here is room for a dissenting opinion. De Jonge's view is supported

---

6. This does not imply that Jesus expressly connected Daniel 7 with Isaiah 53 (see above, pp. 30-33). Both passages speak of a suffering righteous servant who is exalted by God because of his loyalty.

7. See H. J. de Jonge, "The Historical Jesus' View of Himself and his Mission," in M. C. de Boer, ed., *From Jesus to John: Essays on Jesus and New Testament Christology in Honour of Marinus de Jonge* (JSNTSup 84; Sheffield: Sheffield Academic Press, 1993) 21-37 (especially p. 31, n. 1) and also his "De oorsprong van de verwachting van Jezus' komst," in H. J. de Jonge and B. W. J. de Ruyter, eds., *Totdat hij komt: Een discussie over de wederkomst van Jezus Christus* (Baarn: Ten Have, 1995) 9-36. H. J. de Jonge is followed by J. Holleman, *Resurrection and Parousia: A Traditio-Historical Study of Paul's Eschatology in 1 Corinthians 15* (NovTSup 84; Leiden: Brill, 1996); see Chapter 6, "The Expectation of Jesus' Parousia," especially 115-22.

in the interesting section on "Jesus und der Menschensohn" in Helmut Merklein's *Jesu Botschaft von der Gottesherrschaft*.[8] Merklein, too, puts much emphasis on Luke 12:8-9, par. Matt. 10:32-33 and concludes that in the most original version of this saying Jesus and the Son of Man were closely connected, but not identified. Now in Dan. 7:13-14 the "one like a son of man" receives sovereignty, glory, and kingly power forever (cf. verses 18, 22, 27); comparison with Dan. 2:34, 44 shows that God's kingly rule is meant. *1 Enoch* and *4 Ezra* express this aspect of the one like a human being in their own way.[9] Hence Merklein is able to explain the close connection between Jesus and the Son of Man as that between the representative of God's sovereign rule on earth and his heavenly counterpart. God's rule, decreed and realized in heaven (that is how Merklein interprets Luke 10:18) will soon be manifested on earth by the Son of Man. Those who accept Jesus' message will be accepted by the Son of Man.

To scholars who object that in the earliest strands of the tradition words about the Son of Man do not mention God's kingdom, and that words about God's kingdom have no place for the Son of Man,[10] Merklein answers that they may be explained by assuming that, against the background of Daniel 7, the Son of Man concept implies the concept of God's kingly rule, so that the latter need not be mentioned explicitly. The two concepts were closely related, but not, of course, interchangeable. The Son of Man concept, according to Merklein, was, for instance, not suitable to articulate the dynamic presence of God's rule in the words and works of Jesus.

One wonders. As G. R. Beasley-Murray, in his discussion of Luke 12:8-9, has pointed out, "it is self-evident that the kingdom of God that comes in Jesus is the kingdom of God promised for the end of times."[11] If God's kingly rule represented by Jesus is the same as God's kingly rule

---

8. H. Merklein, *Jesu Botschaft von der Gottesherrschaft* (SBS 111; 3d ed. Stuttgart: Katholisches Bibelwerk, 1989) 154-67.

9. See also C. C. Caragounis, *The Son of Man: Vision and Interpretation* (WUNT 38; Tübingen: Mohr Siebeck, 1986).

10. The combination of Mark 8:38 and 9:1 is clearly redactional (see pp. 38 and 66 above) and so is the collocation of the Q texts Matt. 12:28 and 12:32 — *pace* C. C. Caragounis, "Kingdom of God, Son of Man, and Jesus' Self-understanding," *TynBul* 40 (1989) 3-23, 223-28; cf. his *The Son of Man*, 232-43.

11. G. R. Beasley-Murray, *Jesus and the Kingdom of God* (Grand Rapids: Eerdmans; Exeter: Paternoster, 1986) 224-29; quotation on p. 227.

represented by the Son of Man, we may ask whether we are allowed to distinguish between the two representatives. In other words: Will not Jesus' characteristic emphasis on the dynamic presence of God's kingdom have correlated with his use of "Son of Man" to designate himself? This could explain the use of the term to indicate Jesus' authority on earth and even, in the context in Daniel 7 and the application of the model of "the vindication of the suffering righteous servant," its use in connection with his suffering and death. Perhaps by Jesus himself, although the nature of the evidence does not enable us to reach complete certainty.[12]

"Son of Man" in Contemporary Sources and in the Synoptics

It is questionable whether one may speak of a Son of Man concept in Jesus' time, but, as John J. Collins has demonstrated, the *Similitudes of Enoch* (*1 Enoch* 37–71) and *4 Ezra* 13 show common features significant for the interpretation of Daniel 7 in the first century c.e.[13] The "Son of Man" is an individual, not a collective symbol; he is identified in both works with the Messiah; he is preexistent and takes a more active role in the destruction of the wicked than was explicit in Daniel. Henk Jan de Jonge takes this up and goes one step further:[14] the agreements among these first-century works (he adds *Sib. Or.* 5:414-17)[15] and the Gospels are best accounted for by assuming a pre-Christian tradition known to all. I tend to agree, but would put more emphasis on the differences among the various sources. In particular it should be stressed that the *coming* of the Son of Man as judge and ruler is not a fixed element in the supposed common tradition. *Sib. Or.* 5:414 tells us indeed of a "blessed man" coming "from the expanses of heaven" (cf. vv. 108, 158). *4 Ezra* 13:3, however, introduces "a figure

---

12. See above, Chapter 2, pp. 18-23.

13. J. J. Collins, "The Son of Man in First-Century Judaism," *NTS* 38 (1992) 448-65, esp. 464-65; see now his *The Scepter and the Star: The Messiahs of the Dead Sea Scrolls and Other Ancient Literature* (New York: Doubleday, 1995) 173-94.

14. See his publications mentioned above in n. 7.

15. The *Similitudes of Enoch* are now usually dated somewhere in the first century c.e. and *Sibylline Oracles* 5 toward the end of that century. *4 Ezra* is definitely post–70 c.e.

of a man" coming out of the sea (cf. v. 5). This figure is "he whom the Most High has been keeping for many ages, through whom he will deliver his creation" (vv. 25-26). Finally v. 32 specifies: "then my servant will be revealed (Latin: *revelabitur*), whom you saw as a man coming up from the sea (Latin: *ascendentem*)."[16] The *Similitudes of Enoch* speak of an appearance/revelation of the Son of Man in order to judge on behalf of God, seated on his throne of glory. So, for instance, in 69:29: ". . . for that Son of Man has appeared and has sat on the throne of his glory, and everything evil will pass away and go from before him. . . ."[17] Here we should bear in mind that Dan. 7:9 speaks of thrones that are set in place and about the Ancient of Days taking his place on his throne. Later the "one like a son of man" is seen as "coming with the clouds of heaven," that is, as *approaching* the Ancient of Days in order to be presented to him, before receiving everlasting dominion, glory, and kingship (vv. 13-14); his enthronement is, however, not actually described. The plural "thrones" in v. 9 has led to much speculation from an early time onward.[18]

This variety in the descriptions of the activities of the Son of Man may throw some light on the different expressions in the Son of Man texts in the Synoptics. As we have seen, Q (in Luke 12:39-40, par. Matt. 24:43-44) and Mark (8:38; 13:26-27; 14:62) describe a *coming* of the Son of Man, to judge and to save. Mark uses the imagery of Dan. 7:13 to indicate a movement *from heaven to earth*.

Other Q passages (Luke 17:24, 26, 30; Luke 12:8-9, par. Matt. 10:32-33), however, do *not* use the word "coming" to describe the appearance of the Son of Man for judgment. In Luke 22:28-30, par. Matt. 19:28 (cf. Mark 10:35-40, par. Matt. 20:20-23) Jesus acts as ruler and judge together with the Twelve, sitting on thrones — see Dan. 7:9 (cf. Matt. 25:31; Rev. 20:4; and the references to the "sitting at the right hand" in Ps. 110:1). If we combine this with passages dealing with the future coming/manifestation of God's reign (see Chapter 5), we may surmise that *at the earliest stage of the tradition* the prevalent notion inspired by Daniel 7 was the identification of Jesus as Son of Man,

16. Translations taken from M. E. Stone, *Fourth Ezra* (Hermeneia; Minneapolis: Fortress, 1990).

17. Translation taken from M. A. Knibb, *The Ethiopic Book of Enoch*, vol. 2 (Oxford: Clarendon, 1978).

18. See J. J. Collins, *Daniel* (Hermeneia; Minneapolis: Fortress, 1993) 300-301.

expected *to be manifested* as ruler and judge at the moment of God's definitive intervention in order to establish his sovereign rule on earth.

Jesus himself may have envisaged his vindication as messenger of the kingdom in this way. It is unlikely that he, present as inaugurator of the kingdom of God, at the same time announced his coming as the Son of Man from heaven.[19] It is quite conceivable and even probable, however, that he expected to appear as Son of Man, ruling and judging on God's behalf when God's sovereign rule which he had announced would be fully manifest in heaven and on earth. This hypothesis (and it cannot be more given the nature of our evidence) does justice to the sayings on the kingdom of God as well as to (at least an important part of) those on the Son of Man, all specifically connected with Jesus in the Gospel tradition.[20]

Whether and how this view on vindication was, in the mind of Jesus and in that of his followers during his mission, combined with other notions, like resurrection or exaltation, is difficult to determine. After Jesus' death his followers realized that his personal vindication (viewed as resurrection) and the complete breakthrough of the kingdom (bringing about his manifestation in the form of a coming from heaven, the final judgment, and the resurrection of all believers) were two separate events, though directly and intrinsically linked. They realized that they lived in an interim period and adjusted their theology, christology,

---

19. A point strongly emphasized by both H. J. de Jonge and J. Holleman.

20. One may compare the views expressed in two older studies, those by T. F. Glasson, *The Second Advent: The Origin of the New Testament Doctrine* (3d ed.; London: Epworth, 1963) and by J. A. T. Robinson, *Jesus and His Coming: The Emergence of a Doctrine* (London: SCM, 1957). Following lines of argumentation often quite different from those used in the present study, these two scholars try to prove that Jesus never spoke about his parousia in power. They are clearly under the influence of views like those expressed by C. H. Dodd in his well-known study *The Parables of the Kingdom*. So Robinson writes: ". . . we have found nothing requiring us to suppose that Jesus envisaged a second such moment of the Son of Man, beyond and separate from the culmination of the ministry which he came to fulfill" (p. 82). Among recent books on the subject, we may mention V. Hampel, *Menschensohn und historischer Jesus: Ein Rätselwort als Schlüssel zum messianischen Selbstverständnis Jesu* (Neukirchen: Neukirchener Verlag, 1990). This very detailed traditio-historical study of the Son of Man sayings in the Synoptic Gospels reaches conclusions comparable to those reached in the sketch given in Chapters 5–7. Hampel goes into much more detail, however, distinguishing between authentic and inauthentic words of Jesus and delineating a number of different stages in early Christian tradition.

and ethics accordingly. If Jesus reckoned with an interim (Mark 14:25 could point in that direction), it must have been a very short period of transition. The ethical exhortations found in the passages about the parousia recorded above in Chapter 6 presuppose a longer period and hence date from a later time.

CHAPTER 8

Jesus as Messiah and Son of God

We now return to a another question that was left open at the end of Chapter 3. We found that Jesus assigned to himself a central role in the coming of God's rule on earth, not only as a herald but as one who inaugurated it, and we concluded that this implies a christology. We then asked: to what extent did this lead to the use of explicit christological designations in the circle of his disciples during his wanderings in Galilee and Judea, or in his own views about his mission?

Implicit and Explicit Christology

Scholars tend to be very cautious in their answer to the question whether Jesus allowed himself to be called Messiah, or assumed any other designation used for persons playing a role in God's deliverance. This is particularly clear in the case of Rudolf Bultmann, who, though conceding that Jesus' call to decision implies a christology, was disinclined to investigate the continuity between the period before and after Easter in this highly important issue. It was the kerygma of the early Church that transformed the Proclaimer into the Proclaimed. Bultmann's pupil Günther Bornkamm called Jesus unique, in the sense that he claimed to come with God's definite offer and appeal; yet Jesus did not claim any messianic titles for himself.[1] An important argument for the theory

1. See also R. Leivestad, *Jesus in His Own Perspective: An Examination of His*

that Jesus did not use any *Hoheitstitel* is that such titles would have hedged in and, indeed, fixed Jesus' eschatological uniqueness, his claim to speak directly on behalf of God.[2]

This opinion is also found outside the Bultmannian school. Well known is Eduard Schweizer's description of Jesus as the man who fits no formula *("der Mann, der alle Schemen sprengt")*, leading to the conclusion that "in any case Jesus did not assume any current title with an exalted meaning." He adds: "Jesus keeps all the possibilities open; he refuses to use titles, which of necessity define and delimit, to make God's free action an object of human thought, placing it at the disposal of human mind."[3]

Yet there is also another aspect, well brought out by Ferdinand Hahn when he identified as the real secret of Jesus' mission his inner certainty that he stood in a very special relationship to God as his Father.[4] Very interesting and in a way typical of much modern scholarship is Helmut Merklein's approach in his article "Jesus, Künder des Reiches Gottes."[5] On the one hand, he says, it is clear that a decision

---

Sayings, Actions, and Eschatological Titles (Minneapolis: Augsburg, 1987) 120: "It is doubtful that there is any authentic tradition which makes the person of Jesus central, to the extent that it is *he* who acts as savior or judge, and it is *he* upon whom people's fate depends. That which determines salvation or condemnation is whether one receives the message of the Kingdom of God and becomes obedient to God, not whether one associates with the man Jesus."

2. For a short survey of the views of Bultmann and his pupils, see M. de Jonge, *Jesus, The Servant-Messiah* (New Haven: Yale University Press, 1991) 21-26. For the views expressed in this paragraph, see especially R. Bultmann, "The Primitive Christian Kerygma and the Historical Jesus," in C. E. Braaten and R. A. Harrisville, eds., *The Historical Jesus and the Kerygmatic Christ* (Nashville: Abingdon, 1964) 15-42, a translation of a lecture held in 1960; and G. Bornkamm, *Jesus of Nazareth* (New York: Harper and Row, 1960), a translation of *Jesus von Nazareth* (Stuttgart: Kohlhammer, 1956).

3. E. Schweizer, *Jesus* (London: SCM; Richmond: John Knox, 1971) 21-22. In the German original, *Jesus Christus im vielfältigen Zeugnis des Neuen Testaments* (Munich and Hamburg: Siebenstern Taschenbuch, 1968) 25-26: "So oder so hat Jesus jedenfalls keinen gängigen Titel im Sinne einer Hoheitsaussage aufgenommen" but "Jesus hielt das Feld offen, ohne durch Titel, die notwendig immer fixieren und abschliessen, Gottes freies Handeln so zum Objekt menschlichen Denkens werden zu lassen, dass dieses darüber verfügen könnte."

4. F. Hahn, "Methodische Überlegungen zur Rückfrage nach Jesus," in K. Kertelge, ed., *Rückfrage nach Jesus: Zur Methodik und Bedeutung der Rückfrage nach dem historischen Jesus* (QD 63; Freiburg: Herder, 1974) 11-77.

5. Most easily found in H. Merklein, *Studien zu Jesus und Paulus* (WUNT 43;

regarding the message of God's kingdom leads to a decision regarding Jesus as proclaimer and representative of the kingdom. The Lord's Prayer (Luke 11:2-4, par. Matt. 6:9-13) shows that the prayer for the coming of the kingdom is directly connected with the freedom to address God as Father. Jesus addresses God as Father and teaches his disciples to do the same. A new era has begun, and at the heart of it is this special, intimate relationship between Jesus and his Father.

On the other hand, Merklein is of the opinion that an explicit christology making use of messianic titles did not originate before Easter, the event which made it clear that God had inaugurated a new era. He immediately adds, however, that this theory does not exclude but rather assumes that such an explicit christology presupposes Jesus' word and work and the eschatological authoritative claim inherent to it.[6]

I think there is room for a different approach. The use of the terms *implicit* and *explicit* is helpful insofar as it expresses the element of continuity in the positive response to Jesus before and after Easter. But if we think of explicit christology primarily as christology of titles, and titles as fixed concepts, as unequivocal terms defining Jesus' exact role in God's dealings with Israel and the world, then we are on the wrong track. Anyone studying the use of the so-called *Hoheitstitel* within and outside Judaism is immediately struck by the diverse ways in which they are used in a variety of literary and historical contexts.[7] Certain terms stand for different combinations of traditional concepts (often connected with certain texts from scripture), adapted to the specific situations of the authors or of their readers. I do not see why Jesus should

---

Tübingen: Mohr Siebeck, 1987) 127-16; see especially pp. 138, 141-42, and 151-52. Compare also his *Jesu Botschaft von der Gottesherrschaft* (SBS 111; 3d ed.; Stuttgart: Katholisches Bibelwerk, 1989) 84-91.

6. Merklein, *Jesu Botschaft von der Gottesherrschaft*, 147-57.

7. See, e.g., the three christologies of the New Testament that take the titles as their starting point: O. Cullmann, *The Christology of the New Testament* (2d ed.; Philadelphia: Westminster, 1963), a translation of *Die Christologie des Neuen Testaments* (Tübingen: Mohr Siebeck, 1957); F. Hahn, *The Titles of Jesus in Christology: Their History in Early Christianity* (London: Lutterworth; New York: World, 1969), a translation of *Christologische Hoheitstitel: Ihre Geschichte im frühen Christentum* (FRLANT 83; Göttingen: Vandenhoeck & Ruprecht, 1963); and R. H. Fuller, *The Foundations of New Testament Christology* (London: Lutterworth; New York: Charles Scribner's Sons, 1965).

not have clarified his own ideas about his mission, meditating in silence, praying to his God, speaking to his disciples, with the help of terms used to denote special servants of God in Israel's expectations of the future — and why he should not have applied them to his particular situation in a highly individual way.

The term *Son of Man,* as noted in Chapter 7, was not used as a proper title in contemporary Judaism, nor did Jesus use it as a title for himself. Yet it is likely that what was related about "one like a son of man" in Daniel 7 deeply influenced Jesus' thought about his mission and his destiny. His use of the term as a cryptic self-designation betrays a highly individual interpretation of an apocalyptic concept found in the scriptures.

A second remark is in order. The more stress is laid on the continuity between the eschatological expectations of Jesus' followers after Easter and those before, including the conviction that God's kingdom was already dynamically present in the words and deeds of the earthly Jesus, the less likely it becomes that there was a clear discontinuity in the use of christological designations. Even during his lifetime, did Jesus' unique claim to authority not ask for explicit statements, both on the part of his followers and on his own part? If an incipient explicit christology is plausible in theory, are there any indications that it did in fact exist, and that Jesus himself admitted its legitimacy?

Jesus, the Messiah

The word *Messiah* — or, literally, "anointed one" — is frequently used as a general designation for God's final envoy on earth at the inauguration of a new era,[8] but this seems to me to lead to confusion. The

---

8. So also recently G. R. Beasley-Murray, *Jesus and the Kingdom of God* (Grand Rapids: Eerdmans; Exeter: Paternoster, 1986) at the end of an interesting excursus, "The Relation of Jesus to the Kingdom of God in the Present" (pp. 144-46). Here he calls Jesus the "Champion or Contender for the Kingdom of God" (Mark 3:27), "Initiator of the Kingdom" (Matt. 11:12), "Instrument of the Kingdom" (Matt. 12:28), "Representative of the Kingdom of God" (Luke 17:20-21), "Mediator of the Kingdom" (Mark 2:18-19), "Bearer of the Kingdom" (Matt. 11:5), and "Revealer of the Kingdom" (Matt. 13:16-17). He concludes, "Since we would do well to have a term to denote the manifold function of Jesus with respect to the kingdom of God, and since the title *Messiah* is the

term *anointed one* occurs surprisingly seldom in Jewish sources around the beginning of the Common Era. If it is used at all to refer to someone playing a role in God's final intervention, it denotes an ideal Davidic king. Only at Qumran is the term connected a few times with the awaited high priest, and also once with a future prophet. It is not at all self-evident that the word *christos* should have become the central term to be used for Jesus in early Christianity.[9]

At what stage did it become so important? About half the oc-currences of the term in the New Testament are found in the letters of Paul. Here, as Nils A. Dahl has shown, it is seldom used with a technical meaning.[10] The designation Christ "receives its content not through a previously fixed conception of messiahship but rather from the person and work of Jesus Christ." Already before Paul, Jesus was called *christos*, particularly in connection with the formula "Christ died for us/you." This appellation is also found in double formulas speaking about Jesus' death and resurrection (e.g., 1 Cor. 15:3-5; cf. vv. 12-19). And, in general, *christos* stands for what is believed and proclaimed about Jesus, as "the gospel" centering around his death and resurrection.

How then did this term come to be connected with Jesus' death and resurrection? Many have accepted Dahl's answer in yet another

---

acknowledged umbrella term to denote the representative of the kingdom, it is difficult to avoid appropriating it for Jesus" (p. 146). Comparable is P. Pokorny's use of the term. Commenting on the fact that the expectation of the resurrection of many was fulfilled in the resurrection of one person, Jesus, he says: "It follows that everybody's future is dependent on this man. The concretisation implies the representative status of this one person, as the simple statements of faith already indicate. . . . If only one person has risen, he must be the Messiah." See his *The Genesis of Christology: Foundations for a Theology of the New Testament* (Edinburgh: Clark, 1987) 138.

9. See my articles "The Use of the Word 'Anointed' in the Time of Jesus," *NovT* 8 (1966) 132-48, and "The Earliest Christian Use of *Christos:* Some Suggestions," *NTS* 32 (1986) 321-43, now in my *Jewish Eschatology, Early Christian Christology, and the Testaments of the Twelve Patriarchs: Collected Essays* (ed. H. J. de Jonge; NovTSup 63; Leiden: Brill, 1991) 102-24. What follows in this section can be found in more detail in the latter article; cf. my *Christology in Context: The Earliest Christian Response to Jesus* (Philadelphia: Westminster, 1988) 166-67, 208-11.

10. N. A. Dahl, "The Messiahship of Jesus in Paul," in *Jesus the Christ: The Historical Origins of Christological Doctrine* (ed. D. Juel; Minneapolis: Fortress, 1991) 15-25, a translation of "Die Messianität Jesu bei Paulus," in *Studia Paulina in Honorem Johannis de Zwaan* (Haarlem: Bohn, 1953) 83-95. The quotation is from p. 17.

influential article, "The Crucified Messiah."[11] As Dahl aptly points out, "from the discovery of the empty tomb (if it is historical) and from the appearances of the Resurrected One it could be inferred that Jesus lives and is exalted to heaven. But his resurrection would not necessarily mean that he is the Messiah." He continues: "If he was crucified as an alleged Messiah, then — but only then — does faith in his resurrection necessarily become faith in the resurrection of the Messiah. In this way the distinctiveness of the Christian idea of the Messiah, in contrast to the Jewish, was given from the outset."[12] Mark 15 tells us that Jesus was crucified as "King of the Jews" — that is, as one pretending to be the Messiah (see also Mark 14:61-62).

Dahl does not think that Jesus ever used this title for himself. But many of his more ardent followers certainly did. With Bornkamm, says Dahl, we should speak "not of Jesus' non-messianic history before the passion" but rather of "a movement of broken messianic hopes." It is not at all strange that the messianic hopes of Jesus' followers and his sovereign attitude to the law and Jewish customs, coupled with severe criticism of the Jewish establishment, should have led the authorities to accuse him of royal-messianic claims. And Jesus "could not deny the charge that he was the Messiah without thereby putting in question the final, eschatological validity of his whole message and ministry." By not denying it, he accepted the cross; "willingness to suffer is implicit in Jesus' behavior and attitude throughout his preaching."

Dahl's caution is to be commended, but the weak point in his reconstruction is his theory that it was Jesus' opponents who made his messiahship the central question and forced Jesus to accept the charge "by his silence, if not in any other way," as Dahl puts it (p. 34). In his view, only their accusation and Jesus' reaction to it led to the

---

11. In Dahl, *Jesus the Christ*, 27-47. The essay was first published as "Der gekreuzigte Messias," in H. Ristow and K. Matthiae, eds., *Der historische Jesus und der kerygmatische Christus* (Berlin: Evangelische Verlagsanstalt, 1960) 149-69.

12. Dahl, *Jesus the Christ*. The quotations are from p. 38. On the same page he writes: "Jewish messianic expectations do not explain the meaning of the name 'Messiah' assigned to Jesus. Neither can it be said that the title 'Messiah' is the necessary contemporary expression for the conviction that Jesus is the eschatological bringer of salvation. This is no more valid than the older assertion that messiahship was the necessary garb for the archetypal religious self-consciousness of Jesus." The quotations below can be found on pp. 42-43.

adoption of the *christos* title in early Christianity and to its obtaining a central position, directly connected with Jesus' death and resurrection.

I must confess that I find it difficult to accept that Jesus' opponents were able to make messiahship the decisive issue, while Jesus himself avoided this designation and discouraged his followers from using it in connection with him.[13] It is not so easy, however, to demonstrate that he did accept the title Messiah.

The term *christos* is not found in the sayings that can be attributed to Q, and it occurs only a few times in the Gospel of Mark. Among the crucial instances is Peter's confession, "You are the Messiah/Christ" in 8:29, said to be elicited by Jesus himself. It constitutes a turning point in Mark's narrative, after the description of Jesus' activity in Galilee as a unique preacher, teacher, and exorcist at the turn of the ages. Jesus does not contradict this confession but commands his disciples to keep it secret (v. 30). The first of the three predictions of Jesus' suffering, death, and resurrection follows immediately (v. 31) with the designation "Son of Man." For Mark the confession "Jesus is the Christ" presupposes the entire story of Jesus' death, resurrection, and finally the parousia (v. 38). Jesus declares this openly in 14:61-62 in answer to the high priest's question, "Are you the Christ, the Son of the Blessed?" At that crucial moment, facing death, Jesus replies: "I am; and you will see the Son of Man sitting at the right hand of power, and coming with the clouds of heaven." Earlier in the story Jesus praises the faith of the blind beggar Bartimaeus, whom he heals and accepts as his follower after Bartimaeus has addressed him as "Son of David" (10:46-52). At Jesus' entry into Jerusalem he is greeted as one "who comes in the name of the Lord" and associated with "the kingdom of our father David that is coming" (11:9-10). In 12:35-37 Jesus introduces the equation of the Messiah with the son of David as an opinion typically held by the scribes. Referring to Ps. 110:1, he points out that David calls the Messiah "Lord." Although he does not explicitly refer to himself as the Messiah, readers of Mark will immediately note that Ps. 110:1 quoted here is also alluded to in Mark 14:61-62. For Mark Jesus is the Messiah, Son of David. He works on earth as a prophet, teacher, and exorcist; and in the future, after God has vindicated him, he will exercise the functions of the one like a son of man in Daniel

13. So also Leivestad, *Jesus in His Own Perspective*, 95-96.

7. Moreover, for Mark he is Son of God (8:38; 14:61-62; and other texts).[14]

The question remains, however, whether Mark's presentation of Jesus' reaction to the title *christos* reflects Jesus' own attitude or the early christology also expressed in the early pre-Pauline formulas. It is important to remember that Isa. 11:1-5, "The Spirit of the LORD shall rest upon him, the spirit of wisdom and understanding, the spirit of counsel and might, the spirit of knowledge and the fear of the LORD," had exercised a considerable influence on Jewish expectation concerning the coming royal Son of David. A very conspicuous example is *Psalm of Solomon* 17, often (one-sidedly) referred to as a typical example of the earthly and nationalistic messianic expectation. In the last part of the psalm (vv. 30-45), the king is portrayed as "strong with holy spirit, wise in the counsel of understanding with strength and righteousness" (v. 37).[15]

In the Old Testament David is not only king but also psalmist, prophet, and exorcist. In 1 Sam. 16:1-13 we hear how, immediately after Samuel had anointed him, "The Spirit of the LORD came mightily upon David from that day forward" (v. 13). The Spirit of the LORD departs from Saul, and it is David who by singing hymns makes the evil spirit that torments the king depart (1 Sam. 16:14-23). In the introduction to the last words of David (2 Sam. 23:1-7), he is called, among other things, "the anointed of the God of Jacob," and David is recorded as saying "The Spirit of the LORD speaks by me" (vv. 1-2).

Josephus, *Ant.* 6.166-68 describes David's exorcisms; Pseudo Philo, *Liber Antiquitatum Biblicarum* 59-60 mentions new Davidic psalms in this connection, as does the *Psalms Scroll* from Qumran Cave 11. This last source also includes a list of "David's Compositions" that not only mentions an enormous number of psalms and hymns but also specifies that David composed four "songs for making music for the stricken." All his compositions were spoken "through prophecy given to him from before the Most High" (11QPs[a], "David's Compositions," lines 9-11). In Mark 12:36 and in Acts 1:16 and 4:25 David is also said to have spoken through the Holy Spirit, and in Acts 2:30 he is called a prophet.

---

14. Cf. the ancient formula in Rom. 1:3-4: "descended from David according to the flesh and designated Son of God in power according to the Spirit of holiness by his resurrection from the dead."

15. Cf. M. A. Chevallier, *L'Esprit et le Messie dans le Bas-Judaisme et le Nouveau Testament* (Paris: Presses Universitaires de France, 1958). See also pp. 45-49 above.

Mark's characterization of Jesus' activity on earth as prophet, teacher, and exorcist as that of "the Christ, Son of David" is very much in line, then, with the picture of David found in parts of the Old Testament and in some Jewish sources, as well as with certain expectations concerning the future ideal Son of David. The evangelist separates prophecy and exorcism from the royal aspects of the Messiah's activity, however; the latter are specifically connected with the period *after* Jesus' earthly life, when he will exercise royal power in the context of the realization of God's sovereign rule on earth (8:38–9:1; 14:62).

If Jesus' messiahship became an issue at his trial before Pilate only because the designation "Messiah" had earlier been used in connection with Jesus, and probably by Jesus himself, it is quite possible that Mark's interpretation is accurate. Jesus may have understood himself as a prophetic Son of David called to proclaim the gospel and exorcise demons in order to inaugurate God's kingdom, and destined to hold full royal power in the near future. If so, he could regard himself as the Lord's anointed like David, not only in the future, but already during his prophetic work in Galilee.[16] This is how his disciples saw him, as Mark's clearly stylized, prototypical story of Peter's confession seeks to make clear. Jesus' messiahship could be and indeed was misunderstood by some of his followers and many of his opponents alike, but there is no reason to deny that he probably did regard himself as the Lord's anointed in the sense indicated.

Definitive proof cannot be adduced. But this reconstruction also allows for continuity in the use of the designation Messiah before and after Easter. It is certainly one-sided, if not wrong altogether, to connect the title Messiah exclusively with the display of royal power and then to state that Jesus could be called Messiah only after his vindication by means of his resurrection.[17] The convictions gained at Easter affirmed

16. Leivestad, *Jesus in His Own Perspective*, 99-100, pointing only to 1 Sam. 16:13, does not go far enough when he speaks of Jesus as *messias designatus*. David was anointed long before he assumed his kingdom "in power"; he is clearly "the Lord's anointed" from the very moment Samuel has anointed him (1 Sam. 16:6-13).

17. Helmut Merklein is of this opinion, together with many other scholars; see "Die Auferweckung Jesu und die Anfänge der Christologie," in *Studien zu Jesus und Paulus*, 221-46, esp. 224-36. According to Merklein, the oldest explicit christology connected resurrection and enthronement (Mark 14:61-62; Rom. 1:3-4; 1 Thess. 1:9-10; Acts 2:32-36; 13:33). Ferdinand Hahn went even farther and assumed that the title Messiah was originally connected with the parousia (see *The Titles of Jesus in Christology*, 162).

earlier belief in Jesus as Christ as well as expectations concerning his own future and the future of those connected with him. The paradox that the Messiah sent to Israel had been put to death on the cross made an explanation of his death a matter of urgency, as we have seen. This Messiah was, indeed, a servant-Messiah in a very special sense.

Our difficulty is to explain this very special Christian use of the term for Jesus in light of the Jewish material. In contemporary Judaism the prevailing notion was that of a Davidic king, but this king was not necessarily a purely military and political figure. As we have seen in Chapter 4, the *Psalms of Solomon* highlight his obedience to God's will, his wisdom, and his guidance by the Spirit (*Ps. Sol.* 17:37; cf. Isa. 11:1-5). If we connect this with biblical and early Jewish traditions that bring out charismatic features in the activities of king David, we may venture the hypothesis that not only did the tradition presented by Mark see Jesus as a prophetic son of David, but Jesus already regarded himself as such an "anointed one." This was not always correctly understood by his followers, and it was definitely misunderstood by his opponents; this led to his crucifixion as "King of the Jews," a political Messiah.

The weakness of the reconstruction briefly sketched above is, as Wayne Meeks has pointed out, that in the sources at our disposal the prophetic and wisdom elements are subsumed under the general umbrella of kingship.[18] And because there is nothing clearly royal in the mission of Jesus as a prophet, teacher, and exorcist, Meeks remains skeptical that Jesus regarded himself as a prophetic son of David. Henk Jan de Jonge arrives at the same conclusion along a partly different way.[19] He strongly emphasizes that after Jesus' death there was no special historical impulse to use the designation "anointed one" for Jesus; it would never have been used so frequently, if it had not been connected with him earlier. And if Jesus, a clearly nonroyal figure, had no reason to use the term, it must have been introduced by some of his followers who regarded Jesus as a potential political leader and royal redeemer of Israel, against his own intentions. This would have involved only *some*

18. W. A. Meeks, "Asking Back to Jesus' Identity," in M. C. de Boer, ed., *From Jesus to John: Essays on Jesus and New Testament Christology in Honour of Marinus de Jonge* (JSNTSup 84; Sheffield: Sheffield Academic Press, 1993) 38-50, esp. 46-48.

19. H. J. de Jonge, "The Historical Jesus' View of Himself and His Mission," in de Boer, ed., *From Jesus to John*, 21-37, esp. 23-29.

of his followers, because the designation "Christ" is not found in Q and occurs only a few times in Mark.

Meeks rejects my solution of a vexed problem as unconvincing but does not offer an alternative. His and de Jonge's point about *Psalms of Solomon* 17 and the texts about David is right. I have to assume here an unparalleled, highly personal view of Jesus on what the Son of David/Messiah was meant to be. Such an assumption remains hazardous, because this view is nowhere expressed clearly and has to be read between the lines.[20] I ventured my proposal only because I did not (and still do not) see any other way out of the impasse. The hypothesis put forward by de Jonge presents difficulties. How did the belief of only part of Jesus' followers, falsified by Jesus' ignominious death on the cross, lead to the general and very specific Christian use of the designation "Christ"?

Let me, with due caution, adduce two arguments that may support the hypothesis put forward in my book *Jesus, The Servant-Messiah*. First, I would like to point out that *Psalms of Solomon* 17 relates the activity of the expected anointed Son of David with the final manifestation of God's rule in Israel and on the entire earth. As we have seen, the belief that the kingdom of God had been inaugurated in Jesus' mission may have led to the conviction that he was a wise and perfectly obedient anointed one from the seed of David, led by the Spirit.[21] We may not exclude the possibility that this idea originated in Jesus' own mind, but we shall never be able to prove this conclusively.

Second, with regard to the lack of references to the royal aspects of the Son of David/Messiah in the traditions about Jesus, I would like to point to the difficult passage Mark 12:35-37, which has been interpreted in many different ways. Elsewhere I have tried to show that this passage (in connection with 14:61-62) stresses that Jesus is a Son of David, but that his activity as king belongs to the future.[22] There is an analogy here with the ancient tradition found in Rom. 1:3-4, which

---

20. If we were to appeal to the criterion of dissimilarity at all, our appeal would be dismissed for lack of a clear statement attributed to Jesus on the matter.

21. See p. 48 above.

22. M. de Jonge, "Jesus, Son of David and Son of God," in S. Draisma, ed., *Intertextuality in Biblical Writings: Essays in Honour of B. M. F. van Iersel* (Kampen: Kok, 1989) 142-51, now in my *Jewish Eschatology, Early Christian Christology, and the Testaments of the Twelve Patriarchs: Collected Essays* (ed. H. J. de Jonge; NovTSup 63; Leiden: Brill, 1991) 135-44.

combines Jesus' descent from David and his future rule in power as Son of God. It is, therefore, possible to regard Jesus as Son of David and expect the manifestation of his kingly rule at the final breakthrough of God's kingdom. When this view originated, and whether it may be attributed to Jesus, (again) we do not know.

Jesus as the Son of God

Finally, we must ask if Jesus called himself Son of God and if it is possible to say something more about the special relationship between Jesus and God, whom he is reported to have called his Father.

In the earliest Christian traditions accessible to us, the term "Son of God" is used in different contexts with different connotations. In Gal. 4:4-5 Paul employs an ancient pattern of thought when he writes, "But when the time had fully come, God sent forth his Son, born of woman, born under the law, to redeem those who were under the law, so that we might receive adoption as sons." The ancient kernel is here: "God sent forth his Son in order that . . ." — found in Rom. 8:3-4; John 3:16-17; and 1 John 4:9 as well. It is also reflected in the parable of the vineyard in Mark 12:1-9: "He had still one other, a beloved son; finally he sent him to them" (v. 6). The emphasis is on the unique relationship between God and the Son whom he sends at the turn of the ages in order to bring about a fundamental change in the lives of those who accept him. The nature of that change can be expressed in different terms. For Paul and John, the pattern implies pre-existence, but this is not the case in Mark, where it is combined with the concept of Jesus as God's final envoy rejected by Israel.[23]

In a number of other texts, we find "Son of God" together with "Son of David" or "Messiah" (see Mark 12:35-37; 14:61-62; Rom. 1:3-4). Here "Son of God" is associated especially with the period after the exaltation/resurrection (cf. also in Mark 8:38; 1 Thess. 1:9-10). This is also the case in Acts 13:33-34, where Ps. 2:7 is applied to Jesus' resurrection.[24]

---

23. See also de Jonge, *Christology in Context*, 42-43, 190-94 and pp. 118-19 below.

24. This psalm verse is also quoted in Heb. 5:5 and 1:5 (there together with 2 Sam. 7:14; cf. Luke 1:32-33). See also Acts 2:32-36.

These occurrences of "Son of God" should be seen in the context of the use of the term to denote the Davidic king in the Old Testament texts (2 Sam. 7:11-14; Ps. 2:7; Ps. 89:3-4, 26-27; 1 Chron. 17:13; 22:10; 28:6).[25] The special connection between sonship and resurrection may have been inspired by the prophecy attributed to Nathan in 2 Sam. 7:11-14: "I will raise up your offspring after you . . . I will establish the throne of his kingdom for ever . . . I will be his father, and he shall be my son."[26] But in view of the interpretation of the term "Messiah" outlined above, it seems doubtful that Jesus' sonship would have been regarded as beginning only with his exaltation, even where that is stressed. After Jesus' resurrection, it became evident what he, as Son of David and Messiah, already was; it also became apparent that his reign was to last forever.

Paul and Mark successfully combined this tradition about the royal Son of God with the strand of thought that implies that Jesus was Son of God from the very moment his mission began. In the Passion story Mark, too, incorporates the conception of the exemplary righteous servant as Son of God found in Wisd. 2:12-20; 5:1-7; see Mark 15:29-32 (and especially Matt. 27:39-43) and 15:39 (par. Matt. 27:54; Luke 23:47); he even takes one further important step by attributing the introduction of the term "Son of God" into the story of the Gospel to God himself. It is God who declares, "Thou art my beloved Son" when Jesus is baptized and receives the Spirit (1:10-11), and it is God who confirms this, saying, "This is my beloved Son; listen to him" at the transfiguration (9:7). For Mark, Jesus' sonship is rooted in a special relationship inaugurated by God himself.[27] Human beings may not be aware of it (in fact, Jesus' three most intimate disciples know this only because it is revealed to them at the transfiguration), but the demons recognize the Son of God who is mightier than they themselves (3:11; 5:7; cf. 1:24).

In Mark, Jesus is also portrayed as addressing God as *Abba*,

---

25. Cf. 4QFlor 1:10-14, quoting from 2 Sam. 7:11-14 in connection with the "Branch of David," and the much discussed apocalypse 4Q246.

26. See, e.g., M. Hengel, *The Son of God* (Philadelphia: Fortress; London: SCM, 1976) 63-64, translation of *Der Sohn Gottes* (Tübingen: Mohr Siebeck, 1975) 100-101. Hengel refers here to O. Betz and E. Schweizer.

27. See especially J. D. Kingsbury, *The Christology of Mark's Gospel* (Philadelphia: Fortress, 1983) 60-68. See also Mark 13:32. Mark begins his book with the sentence "The beginning of the gospel of Jesus Christ, the Son of God" (1:1), but here, as is well known, it is doubtful whether "Son of God" is original.

"Father." At Gethsemane he prays: "Abba, Father, all things are possible to thee; remove this cup from me; yet not what I will, but what thou wilt (14:36)." The Aramaic word *abba* was used in early Christian prayers, as Paul shows in Gal. 4:4-7. God sent his Son, he says, in order that we might receive adoption as sons. He continues: "And because you are sons, God has sent the Spirit of his Son into our hearts, crying 'Abba! Father!'" (v. 6; cf. Rom. 8:14-17). We may assume that this reflects an ancient usage, rooted in the tradition that Jesus himself called God "Father" and that he taught his disciples to pray in the same way.[28]

The centrality of the relationship to God as Father is clearly evident in the Lord's Prayer, which belongs to the Q material (Luke 11:2-4, par. Matt. 6:9-13), and it also comes to expression in another important Q passage, Luke 10:21-22 (par. Matt. 11:25-27). This passage, which opens with the words, "I thank thee, Father, Lord of heaven and earth," stresses the unique relationship between the Father and the Son, to whom all real knowledge of God is imparted in order that he may reveal it to those he chooses. I cannot treat this frequently discussed passage in detail here. This much is clear, however: the relationship between Father and Son pictured here goes beyond that of the truly righteous man who is called son of God in Wisd. 2:13, 16-18. It is closer to that between (female) Wisdom and God in Wisd. 8:3-4 (cf. 9:9):

> She glorifies her noble birth by living with God,
> and the Lord of all loves her.
> For she is an initiate in the knowledge of God,
> and an associate in his works.

Jesus is more than a supremely wise and righteous man or the ideal representative of Wisdom on earth. He addresses God as Father and speaks and acts out of his very special union with God. Luke 10:21-22 may represent the very core of Jesus' relationship to God, which goes beyond the use of any special title.[29] Yet there, too, continuity exists

---

28. On the use of *abba* (and the recent research on it), see the excellent contribution of J. A. Fitzmyer, "*Abba* and Jesus' Relation to God," in *A cause de l'évangile: Etudes sur les Synoptiques et les Actes offerts à Dom Jacques Dupont* (Lectio Divina 123; Paris: Cerf, 1985) 15-38.

29. On this see, again, Fitzmyer, "*Abba* and Jesus' Relation to God," esp. 35-38, and also the careful study of the passage by B. M. F. van Iersel, *'Der Sohn' in den synoptischen Jesusworten* (NovTSup 3; 2d ed.; Leiden: Brill, 1964) 146-164.

between the early christology expressed in the words "Jesus is the Son of God" and Jesus' own expression of his relationship to his Father.

Jesus not only announced the kingdom of God; he inaugurated it. This placed him in a unique relationship to God, and he was aware of it when he addressed God as Father. It is probable that he regarded himself as the Messiah and Son of David inspired and empowered by the Spirit. We do not know whether he called himself Son of God, but he certainly spoke and acted as the Son on whom the Father had bestowed everything to be his servant at a supreme moment: the long-awaited turning point in human history.

Jesus, then, had a "christology." But immediately we should add that his christology was fundamentally *theocentric*. In fact, all subsequent early Christian christology remained theocentric. "Christology as Theology" will be the subject of the next two chapters.

CHAPTER 9

Christology and Theology
in the Context of Eschatology:
From Jesus to John

This chapter takes as its starting point a number of observations by Nils A. Dahl in his recent book *Jesus the Christ*.[1] This book contains three essays in which Dahl urges his fellow scholars in the field of New Testament and early Christianity to pay more attention to the ways in which early Christians spoke about God. Many studies have concentrated on christology, but theology proper has been neglected. One essay entirely devoted to this subject is called "The Neglected Factor in New Testament Theology."[2] The theme recurs in the concluding pages of an essay entitled "Trinitarian Baptismal Creeds and New Testament Christology,"[3] and among the many traditions and developments sketched in "Sources of Christological Language" (Dahl's Presidential address at the Paris Meeting of the Studiorum Novi Testamenti Societas in 1978),[4] the topic "Language about God Used in Talk about Jesus" also receives attention. As so often in publications by this author, we have to be content with a number of pertinent remarks that invite further thought and with references to earlier treatments of the subject somewhat neglected by mainstream scholarship.

In all of these essays, Dahl insists that "theological and christological utterances condition one another in a variety of ways" (p. 122). More

---

1. N. A. Dahl, *Jesus the Christ: The Historical Origins of Christological Doctrine* (ed. D. H. Juel; Minneapolis, Fortress, 1991).
2. Ibid., 153-63.
3. Ibid., 165-86.
4. Ibid., 113-36.

specifically, "articulated beliefs about God in contemporary Judaism informed the way early Christians understood the crucifixion of Jesus and related events and experiences. At the same time, faith in the crucified Messiah resulted in a new articulation of language used to speak about God" (p. 158). In fact, "New Testament Christology can be treated properly only if it is related to faith in God, as present in the Jewish Scriptures and in contemporary Judaism, which also had assimilated elements of Greek philosophical monotheism" (pp. 179-180). Two further comments deserve mention. First: "Exclusive biblical monotheism was not called into question but remained the rule for the use of christological language" (p. 132). And second: "Before any explicit Christology emerged, sayings and actions of Jesus had identified him in terms of the coming kingdom of God" (p. 131).

Dahl's challenge deserves a response, or rather a variety of responses from scholars who take seriously the theological aspects of early Christian reflection on Jesus.[5] When early Christians spoke about the nature and the effects of Jesus' mission, they had to speak, at the same time, about his relationship to God. In him God had spoken and acted; he continued to do so and was about to crown his dealings with humanity by fully establishing his rule on earth. The proper framework to keep theology and christology together, it would seem, is eschatology — eschatology in the sense of reflection on God's final, definitive intervention in human history, long expected by many in a variety of ways, and now believed by Jesus' followers to have taken place, or rather to have started taking place, in Jesus Christ.

Hence the title of the present chapter, which should be regarded

---

5. Among those who did so in the past, Dahl mentions G. Delling and W. Thüsing. See the studies of Delling, "MONOS THEOS," "Geprägte Gottesaussagen in der urchristlichen Verkündigung," and "Zusammengesetzte Gottes- und Christusbezeichnungen in den Paulusbriefen," in G. Delling, *Studien zum Neuen Testament und zum hellenistischen Judentum: Gesammelte Aufsätze 1950-1968* (eds. F. Hahn, T. Holtz, N. Walter; Göttingen: Vandenhoeck & Ruprecht, 1979) 391-400; 401-16; 417-24, respectively; and K. Rahner and W. Thüsing, *Christologie — Systematisch und Exegetisch* (QD 55; Freiburg: Herder, 1972); W. Thüsing, *Erhöhungsvorstellung und Parusieerwartung in der ältesten nachösterlichen Christologie* (SBS 42; Stuttgart: Katholisches Bibelwerk, 1970); idem, *Per Christum in Deum: Studien zum Verhältnis von Christozentrik und Theozentrik in den paulinischen Hauptbriefen* (NTAbh 1; 2d ed.; Münster: Aschendorf, 1969). Dahl also mentions A. Wire, "Pauline Theology as an Understanding of God: The Explicit and the Implicit" (Ph.D. diss., Claremont, 1974), which I have not seen.

as an essay in the proper sense of the word, that is, as an (initial) attempt at clarification. The first part of the title could also have been formulated differently, for instance as "Theology as Christology" or "Christology as Theology."[6] Essential is the second part indicating "eschatology" as the uniting factor.

This essay does not limit itself to early christology and theology, from Jesus to Paul, but continues with a discussion of Johannine christology. The Gospel of John deals quite explicitly with the relationship between Father and Son, and it stresses their unity in action. It also speaks about Jesus in such a way that at least some have feared that exclusive monotheism was in danger. Among these were the opponents of Johannine Christianity portrayed as "the Jews." We shall have to investigate how John's statements about Son and Father relate to the typically Johannine eschatology found in the Gospel and the Epistles. The suggested treatment of christology and theology in the context of eschatology will bring out an important element of continuity in the development of early Christian reflection upon Jesus' mission. In this respect this chapter links up with the preceding ones.

From Jesus to Paul

It is apposite to begin with a short survey of our findings in the preceding chapters insofar as they are of importance to the present inquiry. There is a (nearly) general consensus among scholars that Jesus spoke about the speedy revelation and complete realization of God's sovereign rule in his entire creation, and that he claimed that in his own words and actions the kingdom was already breaking through. Characteristic of Jesus' mission was the conviction of the dynamic presence of God's rule inaugurating a complete breakthrough in the near future (Chapter 3).

6. In Rahner and Thüsing, *Christologie*. Thüsing's fifth chapter is called "Christologie und Theo-logie: Die christologisch bestimmte Theo-logie des NT." In an introductory note on p. 133, he states that the time has come to realize that "neutestamentliche Neuansätze der Christologie eine durchgängige Untersuchung und Reflexion des Verhältnisses Jesu zu Gott zur Voraussetzung haben (entsprechend der Sinnrichtung des Lebens Jesu selbst), d.h. eine von der Theo-logie her und auf sie hin konzipierte Christologie."

As we have seen in Chapter 2, the three models used very early among Christians to explain Jesus' death presuppose that already before his death Jesus' followers believed that in his mission he had inaugurated the new era promised by God. Jesus was seen as the final messenger of God to Israel, rejected and killed; as a righteous servant of God, suffering and vindicated; and as a martyr giving his life for those connected with him — and again vindicated by God. In all cases the emphasis is on the finality of Jesus' mission and on the definitive change brought about by it. It may be argued that this element of finality, which was not inherent in traditional Jewish use of any of the models, was brought in because it had been the central issue in Jesus' own message and was fervently believed by his followers.

Jesus' conviction that he played a central role in the coming of God's kingdom, precisely because he not only announced but also inaugurated it, implies a christology. At the same time, however, this cannot have been anything other than a theocentric christology, as we have seen in Chapter 8. The emphasis is on God's initiative, on his decision to inaugurate the kingdom with a view to establishing his sovereign rule in his entire creation in the near future. "Father, hallowed be your name, your kingdom come" (Luke 11:2). "But about that day or hour, no one knows, neither the angels in heaven, nor the Son, but only the Father" (Mark 13:32). To Jesus, and consequently to his followers, the initiative remains with God; hence their tense, short-term expectation of the complete realization of what had already begun.

Luke 11:2 (Q) connects the concentration on God's sovereignty with the trust in him as Father. This connection was characteristic of early Christianity (Gal. 4:4-7; Rom. 8:14-17) and, according to Mark and Q, of Jesus (Mark 14:36; Luke 10:21-22, par. Matt. 11:25-27; cf. Luke 11:9-13, par. Matt. 7:7-11). Addressing God as Father implies intimacy and trust, complete dependence on what he chooses to impart or to accomplish, and obedience to his will. Theocentricity implies centering on God the Father. It was Jesus who, from his own intimate relationship with the Father, invited his disciples to enter into a child-father relationship with God.

Jesus' trust in his Father, together with his conviction that he had been commissioned to inaugurate God's kingdom, must have led to the inner certainty that the complete realization of God's rule would bring the vindication of his message and thereby of his own person and mission. If, as seems very likely, towards the end of his mission Jesus had to reckon seriously with the possibility that the opposition and hostility which he encountered would lead to his violent death, he must have believed that he would be vindicated by God after his death. It is difficult to determine what form he expected this vindication to take. He must have believed that his message about the complete break-through of the kingdom in the near future would be proven true, and that he and his followers would participate in it. In Chapters 5–7 an attempt was made to delineate how he might have envisaged this vin-dication and his future participation in the kingdom.

Jesus' followers, after his death, realized that his personal vindica-tion and the complete breakthrough of the kingdom were two separate events, though directly and intrinsically connected. They were recon-ciled to live in an interim period between the resurrection of Jesus and his parousia, which would bring the final judgment and the resurrection of all believers. The conviction that God had indeed vindicated Jesus, and thereby his message about the inaugurated kingdom, led them to envisage and to experience the period of the "not yet" before the parousia as a time in which the community of the faithful already participated to some extent in the blessings of the kingdom. A number of statements in Paul about the kingdom of God, for instance, connect it with the future (1 Cor. 6:9-10; Gal. 5:19-21; 1 Cor. 15:22-28, 50) and specifically with the parousia (particularly in 1 Thessalonians; see 1:10; 2:11-12, 19; 3:12-13; 4:13-18; 5:23), but he also speaks about the pres-ence of the kingdom in the community of believers. It "does not consist in talk but in power" (1 Cor. 4:20); it is a matter of "righteousness and peace and joy in the Holy Spirit" (Rom. 14:17).[7]

In fact, notwithstanding the discontinuity due to Jesus' departure and his ignominious death on the cross, there is clearly continuity in essentials between the reactions of Jesus' disciples during his life to his message of the inaugurated kingdom and, later, their interpretation of the present in which they lived as the time between Jesus' death and resurrection and his imminent parousia. This continuity has been brought out clearly by Wilhelm Thüsing, who has also argued that, because of it, words connected with the earthly Jesus — like those col-lected in Q — could be regarded as relevant and authoritative in the post-Easter period. Presupposed is the vindication of Jesus, his exalted state in the presence of God, his continued contact with his followers

---

7. See above, pp. 35-36.

on earth through the activity of the Spirit, and his coming in power at the final breakthrough of God's sovereign rule.[8] The role of the vindicated Jesus in God's salvation is duly emphasized, explicit christological statements are formulated, and *Hoheitstitel* tend to stress Christ's power and glory; yet there is an acute awareness that this christocentric faith remains in the last resort directed to God, the Father of Jesus Christ.

This may be illustrated with a few examples of expressions found in the letters of Paul (often going back to pre-Pauline usage), taken from those collected by Gerhard Delling and Wilhelm Thüsing.[9] First, we may notice that among the early formulas expressing the meaning of Jesus' death and resurrection (apart and together),[10] many of those speaking about the resurrection alone mention God, explicitly or implicitly, as the one who raised Jesus (from the dead) — see Rom. 4:24; 8:11; 10:9; 1 Cor. 6:14; 15:15; 2 Cor. 4:14; Gal. 1:1; 1 Thess. 1:10; cf. Col. 2:12; Eph. 1:20; 1 Pet. 1:21. In Rom. 4:24 the phrase "believe in him who raised Jesus our Lord from the dead" follows on the characterization of the faith of Abraham as belief in "the God . . . who gives life to the dead and calls into existence the things that do not exist" in Rom. 4:17 (cf. 2 Cor. 1:9; Heb. 11:19).[11] Paul connects Christian convictions concerning Jesus' resurrection with the (Pharisaic) Jewish belief in God "who gives life to the dead" — see the second of the *Eighteen Benedictions.*

---

8. See particularly Thüsing, *Erhöhungsvorstellung und Parusieerwartung;* on p. 57 he writes: "Die Logien Jesu wurden nicht wie das Vermächtnis eines Verstorbenen tradiert, sondern als Worte des bei Gott lebenden Jesus; der Kern von Q, das heisst eine frühe Sammlung von Herrnworten (die vermutlich schon auf vorösterliche Ursprünge zurückgeht) diente als 'Gefäss' für das Eigentliche und Wichtigste, was die älteste Gemeinde zu sagen hatte. . . . Nähehin diente die Betonung der heilsentscheidenden Sendung (beziehungsweise der 'Exusia') Jesu in Q als Äquivalent für eine Erhöhungsaussage, insofern sie Darstellungsmittel für die Funktion und Machtsstellung des erhöhten Jesus war."

9. For Delling's essays, see note 5 above. Of Thüsing's publications mentioned in the same note, see in particular his *Per Christum in Deum.*

10. See M. de Jonge, *Christology in Context: The Earliest Christian Response to Jesus* (Philadelphia: Westminster, 1988) 33-43.

11. So also G. Delling, "Geprägte Gottesaussagen," 406-7. He compares this expression with various participial phrases about God in the Old Testament. On p. 409 he points to the cases in which a passive form of *egeirein* is used and states that "in der passivischen Fassung sehr wahrscheinlich eingeschlossen ist, dass Gott der ist der Jesus auferweckte." This need not be so; significantly, in two cases of the double formula another verb is used — see 1 Thess. 4:14, "Jesus died and rose again," and Rom. 14:9, "Christ died and lived again."

The emphasis is on God's initiative and action. In a number of the texts just mentioned, God's raising of Jesus is connected with the future resurrection of those who acknowledge Jesus' central position in God's plan of salvation (see Rom. 8:11; 1 Cor. 6:14; 2 Cor. 4:14; 1 Thess. 4:13-18; 1 Corinthians 15 *passim;* cf. Rom. 6:2-11; 2 Cor. 5:14-15; 2 Tim. 2:12; and Rom. 4:24; 10:9).

If we look to the expected completion of God's saving activity, we notice that the Old Testament expression "the day of the Lord" is now connected with Jesus as Lord — so in 1 Cor. 5:5 and 1 Thess. 5:2 ("the day of the Lord"); 1 Cor. 1:8 ("the day of our Lord Jesus Christ"); and 2 Cor. 1:14 ("the day of [our] Lord Jesus"). Hence also the expression "the day of (Jesus) Christ" in Phil. 1:6, 10; 2:16. We already remarked that in 1 Thessalonians the final realization of God's rule is connected with the parousia of Jesus Christ. In all relevant texts (1 Thess. 2:19; 3:13; 4:15; 5:23) he is called Lord. Christians pray for the coming of the Lord (*Maranatha* — 1 Cor. 16:22; cf. 1 Cor. 11:26; Phil. 3:20). Yet this does not mean that Jesus, the Lord, has taken the place of the LORD God. This is brought out clearly by Paul in 1 Cor. 15:20-28. Christ, whose own resurrection guarantees the resurrection of all who are "in Christ" (or: "belong to Christ"), will in the end hand over the kingdom to God the Father (v. 24), for "when all things are subjected to him, then the Son himself will also be subjected to the one who put all things in subjection under him, so that God may be all in all" (v. 28).

In the present, intermediary period between resurrection and parousia, the Lord Jesus is portrayed as "sitting at the right hand of God," an expression derived from Ps. 110:1, an Old Testament text that was very influential in the shaping of early christology.[12] This psalm verse mentions two lords, and early Christians were very much aware that Jesus, the exalted one, remained second to the LORD God. Romans 8:34 speaks about "Christ Jesus, who died, yes, who was raised, who is at the right hand of God, who indeed intercedes for us" in a context that emphasizes God's sustained initiative (vv. 28-39)[13]; nothing and

---

12. See de Jonge, *Christology in Context,* 186-88.

13. We should note in passing Rom. 8:32, where we have a variant of the so-called surrender formula. Usually Jesus is the grammatical subject; he gave himself for others (Gal. 1:4; 2:20; Mark 10:45, par. Matt. 20:28; 1 Tim. 2:6; Titus 2:14). In Rom. 8:32 we find the statement "(God) who did not withhold his own Son, but gave him up for all of us" (cf. Rom. 4:25, where a passive is used).

nobody in earth or in heaven "will be able to separate us from the love of God in Christ Jesus our Lord" (v. 39). The risen Jesus "lives for God" (Rom. 6:9); believers belong to Christ, but "Christ belongs to God" (1 Cor. 3:23); "Christ is the head of every man, and the husband is the head of his wife," but "God is the head of Christ" (1 Cor. 11:3). The relationship between the exalted Jesus and God is very clearly expressed in the hymn in Philippians 2:

> Therefore God also highly exalted him
> and gave him the name above every name,
> so that at the name of Jesus every knee should bend,
> in heaven and on earth and under the earth,
> and every tongue should confess that Jesus Christ is Lord,
> to the glory of God the Father. (vv. 9-11)

Jesus the Lord is often mentioned together with God, particularly in more or less fixed expressions. We need only point to the greeting formula at the beginning of Paul's letters (Rom. 1:7; 1 Cor. 1:3; 2 Cor. 1:2; Gal. 1:3; Phil. 1:2; 1 Thess. 1:1; Phlm. 3; cf. 2 Thess. 1:2; Col. 1:2; Eph. 1:2; 1 Tim. 1:2; 2 Tim. 1:2; Tit. 1:4), in which God is called "our Father" (1 Thess. 1:1: "the Father") and Jesus is referred to as "the Lord Jesus Christ." Believers may call God "our Father," because he is the Father of his Son Jesus Christ, as is made clear in Gal. 4:4-7 (cf. Rom. 8:14-17, 26-29). There is an analogy here with the time before Jesus' death, when it was he who taught his disciples to pray to the Father. Whenever it has to be stressed that God is the creator and the initiator of salvation, as well as the supreme director and goal of all, he is called God the Father — so not only in 1 Cor. 15:20-28 and Phil. 2:9-11 but also in 1 Cor. 8:6:

> yet for us there is one God, the Father,
> from whom are all things and for whom we exist,
> and one Lord, Jesus Christ,
> through whom are all things and through whom we exist.

Or, somewhat differently, there is Paul's wish for the Christians in Rome: "May the God of steadfastness and encouragement grant you to live in harmony with one another, in accordance with Christ Jesus, so that together you may with one voice glorify the God who is the

Father of our Lord Jesus Christ" (Rom. 15:5-6;[14] cf. also v. 7; Phil. 1:11; 1 Thess. 5:23). Jesus' position and activity in the history of God's dealings with humanity are central and crucial in the past, the present, and the future, but all he has done, is doing, and will do serves God's purpose. The goal is that "God may be all in all" (1 Cor. 15:28). All believers are summoned to produce "the harvest of righteousness that comes through Jesus Christ for the glory and praise of God" (Phil. 1:11).

In conclusion, and by way of transition to the next section, we may point to the expression "God sent his Son in order that . . .," which apparently provided a useful pattern of thought in early Christianity. We find it in Gal. 4:4-7; Rom. 8:3-4; Mark 12:1-9; and in John 3:16-17; 1 John 4:9.[15] The "christology of mission" so very typical of Johannine thought presents many variations on this basic theme. Those who use this pattern of thought put emphasis on God's initiative as well as on the close relationship between him and his Son whom he commissions to carry out a mission at the turn of the ages (Mark 12:6: "finally"; Gal. 4:4: "when the fullness of time had come"). Those who accept him are freed from the bondage of the law (Rom. 8:2-4; Gal. 4:5), live in the Spirit as (adopted) children of God (Rom. 8:4; Gal. 4:5-7), and have eternal life through him (John 3:16-17; 1 John 4:9). Those who reject him will be punished, like the wicked tenants whose vineyard will be given to others (Mark 12:9), and will perish (John 3:16).

Paul and John clearly regard the unique relationship between God and his Son as existing already before the Son was sent out on his mission. In Mark the "sending pattern" is combined with that of Jesus as God's envoy to Israel (mentioned above among the models explaining Jesus' death). The word "son" belongs here to the imagery of the parable and, like the word "heir" used by the tenants, it serves to distinguish the person concerned from the "servants" sent out on earlier missions. It emphasizes the son's unique and intimate relationship to the owner of the vineyard, and thereby that of Jesus as Son of

14. Following the translation of G. Delling, "Zusammengesetzte Gottes- und Christusbezeichnungen in den Paulusbriefen," 419.

15. See above, p. 106. On these texts, see particularly E. Schweizer, "Zum religionsgeschichtlichen Hintergrund der 'Sendungsformel' Gal 4,4f.; Röm 8,3f.; Joh 3,16f.; 1 Joh 4,9," *ZNW* 57 (1966) 199-210, also in *Beiträge zur Theologie des Neuen Testaments* (Zürich: Zwingli, 1970) 83-95. See also Schweizer's recent article "Was meinen wir eigentlich wenn wir sagen 'Gott sandte seinen Sohn . . .'?" *NTS* 37 (1991) 204-24.

God over against the prophets sent before him. What is said does not enable the reader to extrapolate anything about the nature of his relationship to God before his mission.[16] In 12:6 the evangelist uses the expression "a beloved son," clearly referring to God's word to Jesus at the beginning of his mission in 1:11 (and to 9:7, where it is repeated). There, too, nothing is said or implied about the period before — God commissions the one most dear to him, his beloved, only son, with his unique mission prepared by John the Baptist, and he equips him with the Holy Spirit (Mark 1:9-13). His message is of crucial importance ("This is my beloved Son, listen to him," Mark 9:7) — as is illustrated in the parable of the wicked tenants.

This "sending pattern" is obviously used in a variety of ways in a variety of contexts. In all applications it speaks about God and the Son in one breath, combining theology and christology.

The Johannine Writings

In the Fourth Gospel the "christology of mission" occupies a very important place.[17] It does not come as a surprise that a number of recent authors who write about the relationship between Jesus Christ and God in Johannine thought pay much attention to it.[18] William

16. So also E. Schweizer, "Was meinen wir eigentlich," 214.

17. See de Jonge, *Christology in Context,* 145-147. M. Hengel, *The Johannine Question* (London: SCM/Philadelphia: Trinity Press International, 1989) 103, speaks of "the 'multiplicity of approaches' which express the one action of God, the sending of the Son for the salvation of the world, in constantly new metaphors and imagery."

18. See C. K. Barrett, "Christocentric or Theocentric? Observations on the Theological Method of the Fourth Gospel," in J. Coppens, ed., *La notion biblique de Dieu: Le Dieu de la Bible et le Dieu des philosophes* (BETL 41; Gembloux: Duculot; Leuven: Leuven University Press, 1976) 361-76; idem, " 'The Father is Greater than I' (Jo 14,28): Subordinationist Christology in the New Testament," in J. Gnilka, ed., *Neues Testament und Kirche: Für Rudolf Schnackenburg* (Freiburg: Herder, 1974) 144-59, now in C. K. Barrett, *Essays in John* (London: SPCK; Philadelphia: Westminster, 1982) 1-18 and 19-36, respectively; J. D. G. Dunn, "Let John Be John," in P. Stuhlmacher, ed., *Das Evangelium und die Evangelien: Vorträge vom Tübinger Symposion 1982* (WUNT 28; Tübingen: Mohr Siebeck, 1983); L. Hartman, "Johannine Jesus-Belief and Mono-theism," in L. Hartman and B. Olsson, eds., *Aspects on the Johannine Literature* (ConBNT 18; Uppsala: Almqvist and Wiksell, 1987) 85-99; W. A. Meeks, "Equal to

R. G. Loader regards it as basic to the structure of the gospel's christology.[19] With regard to the Fourth Gospel, he prefers to speak of a
"revealer envoy christology" developed out of the "sending christology." John 3:16-17 is very near to Gal. 4:4 and Rom. 8:3; but, he
points out, "the form of sending christology we have in John goes
considerably beyond these and is different in the dualism it presupposes, in its soteriology, and above all, in its understanding of the role
of pre-existence."

In the context of the present essay, the question has to be asked
to what extent the specifically Johannine elaboration and (we may say)
intensification of the "christology of mission" have influenced the essentially theocentric thrust of this christological model. There is, after
all, evidence that the Johannine community had to defend itself against
the charge of ditheism and blasphemy — see John 5:17-30; 10:22-39 (cf.
19:7). Another important issue is the combination of this dominant
model with other elements essential to the traditional message about
Jesus, especially his saving death and resurrection, and the crowning of
God's definitive intervention on earth in the near future. On closer
inspection, Johannine christology is not as uniform and consistent as it
sometimes looks; there are also considerable differences between the
Gospel and the First Epistle in this respect. Loader rightly calls the
christology of the Gospel a "christology in development."[20] It is important to determine the nature of this development. We need not doubt
that the Johannine community wanted to bring out what it considered
to be the essential message of Christianity for the particular circumstances in which it found itself. In living tradition, interpretation always
leads to reinterpretation at certain points. Do those aspects of Johannine
christology that — in our view — can only with difficulty be combined
with its central core represent traditional elements that are regarded as
indispensable, but are not (yet) fully integrated, or are they relics not

---

God," in R. T. Fortna and B. R. Gaventa, eds., *The Conversation Continues: Studies in
Paul and John in Honor of J. Louis Martyn* (Nashville: Abingdon, 1990) 308-21; in the
same volume, compare also R. H. Fuller, "Higher and Lower Christology in the Fourth
Gospel," 357-65.

19. W. R. G. Loader, *The Christology of the Fourth Gospel: Structure and Issues*
(BBET 23; 2d ed.; Frankfurt: Peter Lang, 1992). The following quotation is from p. 215.

20. Ibid., 213. He adds, "The potential for greater dominance of the revealer envoy
model, at the expense of other traditions, is already apparent and will be realised in
gnosticism."

(yet) discarded, but without any function?[21] In the present context this question will have to be addressed with regard to the statements concerning future eschatology.

We may begin by looking somewhat more closely at the parallels between Gal. 4:4-5 and Rom. 8:3-4 on the one hand, and John 3:16-17 and 1 John 4:9 on the other. In Paul the purpose of the Son's mission is redemption of "those who were under the law" (Gal. 4:4), that is, redemption "from the curse of the law" (Gal. 3:13), and "to condemn sin in the flesh" (Rom. 8:3). For Paul the Son's mission encompasses his life and his death, as Gal. 3:13 shows, as does Rom. 8:32, which stresses that God gave up *(paredōken)* his own Son for all of us. In John 3:16-17 "giving" *(edōken)* in v. 16[22] stands parallel to "sending" in the next verse; it follows on verses 14 and 15, which speak about the "lifting up" of the Son of Man — an expression that in John refers not only to Jesus' exaltation, but also to the cross (12:32-33). Next, in 1 John 4:9, "God sent his Son into the world so that we might live through him" is followed in v. 10 by ". . . sent his Son to be the atoning sacrifice for our sins." Both Johannine texts speak about "the only Son," linking up with Mark 12:6.

In Gal. 4:4-5 the sending of the Son is connected with the sending of the Spirit in 4:6-7 (cf. Rom. 8:14-17, 23-24). In John the sending/giving of the Spirit takes place at the return of the Son to the Father at the completion of his mission. The Spirit is sent by the Father and the Son, in close cooperation (14:16, 26; 15:26; 16:7); working within the community of believers, he "will teach you everything, and remind you of all that I have said to you" (14:26). Just as the Son is dependent on the Father, the Spirit is dependent on the Son. "He will glorify me, because he will take what is mine and declare it to you. All that the Father has is mine" (16:14-15).[23] Finally, in Paul the activity of the Spirit in the circle of believers is connected with their status as (adopted) sons. John, too, calls believers "children of God" (1:12-13; cf. 3:3-7; 11:52; 1 John 3:1-2; 5:2).[24]

---

21. Or were at least some of them, as is often thought, reintroduced at a later stage in the history of the Johannine community, in order to bring its radical ideas in line with those current in mainline Christianity?

22. Compare the use of the latter verb in the expression "he gave himself" in Gal. 1:4; 1 Tim. 2:6; Tit. 2:14; Mark 10:45.

23. This should, of course, be dealt with in far more detail than is possible here. For a somewhat longer survey of the issues involved, see Loader, *The Christology of the Fourth Gospel,* 85-92.

24. Reserving "children" for believers and using "son" for Jesus.

In Paul and in the Johannine writings, the emphasis is on the salvation, the true life, granted to those who put their trust in what the Son's mission set out to achieve. For Paul it is the beginning of the glory yet to be revealed in the context of the renewal of the entire creation (Rom. 8:12-25). John stresses what happens now: "this is the judgment, that the light has come into the world, and people loved darkness rather than the light because their deeds were evil" (John 3:19). But behind God's sending of the Son lies his love for the world (v. 16); though judgment may be the result, God sent his Son "in order that the world might be saved through him" (v. 17; cf. 6:51; 12:47). Hence the Son may be called "the savior of the world" (4:42). In 1 John this expression is used in 4:14, and the expression "atoning sacrifice for our sins" in 4:10 has a parallel in 2:2, which adds "and not for our sins only, but also for the sins of the whole world." We shall have to return later to the fact that the salvation of the world through the Son is clearly still outstanding.

Turning now to the many other variations on the basic theme "God sent his Son" in the Fourth Gospel, we may single out a few striking examples which show that the evangelist is at pains to emphasize the Son's unity with and dependence upon the Father.[25] Repeatedly, God as sender of the Son is called "the Father" (5:23, 37; 6:44; 8:16, 18; 12:49; 14:24). The Son does nothing "on his own" (5:19, 30; 7:17, 28; 8:28, 42; 12:49; 14:10); he does God's will (4:34; 5:30; 6:38-40), for he has to do/complete God's work (4:34; 5:36; 10:37-38; 14:12; 17:4; cf. 5:17; 9:4). In fact, his works are the works of the Father, and the Father works through him (14:10).

The relationship between Father and Son is one of love (3:35; 5:20; 10:17; 14:21, 31; 15:9; 17:23-26). There is also a continuous link between the two (5:19-20, 30; 8:16, 29; 16:32). We may speak here of "functional unity." The statement "The Father and I are one" in 10:30 explains that Jesus as the good shepherd is able to give eternal life to his sheep, and that no one is able to snatch them out of the Father's hand.[26] He

---

25. On the following, see also Chapter 6, "The Son of God and the Children of God," in M. de Jonge, *Jesus: Stranger from Heaven and Son of God* (SBLSBS 11; Missoula Mont.: Scholars Press, 1977) 141-68. For valuable insights with regard to the cultural and history-of-religions background of John's christology of mission, see especially Jan-A. Bühner, *Der Gesandte und sein Weg im 4. Evangelium* (WUNT 2/2; Tübingen: Mohr Siebeck, 1977) esp. 118-373.

26. This holds true whatever the original reading of v. 29a may have been.

performs his works in his Father's name (vv. 25-30). In the following discussion (vv. 31-39) with the Jews, who accuse him of blasphemy because he makes himself God (v. 33), Jesus introduces the idea of "mutual indwelling": "Believe the works, so that you may know and understand that the Father is in me, and I am in the Father" (10:38; cf. 14:10-11, 20; 17:21-23).[27] In this discourse with the Jews, just as in the earlier one in 5:17-30 (plus vv. 31-46), we hear the reply of the Johannine community to the accusations of Pharisaic Jews of their time. All along Johannine Christians maintain, in good faith, that Jesus did not make himself God (10:33 and 5:18; cf. 19:7) but that, as Son sent by the Father, he was completely obedient to his Father's will and was able to perform the works of the Father.

In the context of Johannine dualism, it is emphasized that the one who was sent came "from above," "from heaven" (3:13, 31; 6:31-58; 8:23), that is, "from God" (6:46; 8:42, 47; 9:16, 33; 13:3; 16:30). These expressions underscore the divine origin and the unique authority of Jesus' words (and actions). We also hear that Jesus came from God in order to return to him again at the completion of his mission. Different Greek verbs are used, all indicating departure.[28] In three cases the verb "to ascend" is used (3:13; 6:62; 20:17) to correspond to an earlier descent (3:13; "to descend" is also used of the bread from heaven, identified with Jesus in 6:33, 38, 41, 42, 50, 51). In fact, as is made clear in the (difficult) verse 3:13, only one, the Son of Man, has ascended to heaven; he is the one who also descended. John's christology of mission claims exclusivity for Jesus;[29] his is a unique mission, beginning and ending with God in heaven.

Jesus the Son, the exemplary envoy, in complete obedience to the will of his Sender, in loving unity with the Father, speaks and acts as the Father. Hence "the Father and I are one" (10:30), and "whoever has seen me has seen the Father" (14:9; cf. 12:45). Yet it is self-evident that "the Father is greater than I" — the Father to whom the Son returns at the completion of his mission (14:31). This can all be explained as an

27. This idea is often connected with that of the mutual indwelling of the Son (and the Father) and the disciples (14:20, 23; 15:2-10; 17:21-23, 26).

28. We find the words *poreuomai* (so 14:2, 3, 12, 28; 16:7, 28), *hypagō* (7:33; 8:14; 13:3; 14:4, 5, 28; 16:5, 10, 17), and *aperchomai* (16:6).

29. Over against claims of Jewish apocalyptic and mystical groups regarding direct knowledge of heavenly mysteries by means of a vision or an ascent to heaven — see, e.g., Dunn, "Let John Be John," 309-39, esp. 323-25.

elaboration and intensification of the christology of mission that John took over from Christian tradition.[30]

It is often claimed that the Johannine christology of mission can only be fully explained when we note how it is combined with the Logos christology of the Prologue (1:1-18). James Dunn, for instance, stresses that "the Fourth Evangelist really did intend his Gospel to be read through the window of the Prologue."[31] For him,

> the key to understanding the Johannine distinctives in his presentation of Jesus as Messiah, Son of God, and Son of Man, is to see these titles primarily as *an elaboration of the initial explicit identification of Jesus as the incarnate Wisdom/Logos* — an identification taken over certainly from earlier Christian tradition, but expounded in John's own distinctive fashion. It is this which alone satisfactorily explains John's repeated emphasis on the direct continuity between Jesus and God from the beginning of time.

In this way theocentricity and monotheism are safeguarded: "Precisely because Wisdom/Logos rather than Son of God is his primary category, he remains a monotheist — for while 'Son' is more fitted to express distinction and relation (as Athanasius realized), 'Logos' by definition better expresses sameness and continuity."

I am not sure that Dunn's theory about the relationship of Logos christology and Son christology is right. In the present context it is sufficient, however, to note that the Logos christology supplements what could less adequately be expressed in a christology of mission — a christology that in itself safeguarded theocentricity.[32] One thing is clear: John speaks about the relationship between God and the Logos/Son before and

---

30. In the Fourth Gospel "I am," too, (without a predicate) is used essentially as a revelatory formula. Jesus is able to reveal himself in the way God reveals himself (see, e.g., Isa. 43:10; Exod. 3:14), because as the Son he speaks and acts in unity with the Father. See de Jonge, *Christology in Context*, 147; Barrett, "Christocentric or Theocentric?" 371-72; Loader, *The Christology of the Fourth Gospel*, 166-67.

31. Dunn, "Let John Be John," 330-37; the quotations below are from p. 331 and p. 335. Compare also his *Christology in the Making: A New Testament Inquiry into the Origin of the Doctrine of the Incarnation* (Philadelphia: Westminster, 1980) 163-250.

32. See also Loader, *The Christology of the Fourth Gospel*, 167-72. On p. 170 he speaks of "the tension between the more strongly ontological orientation of the logos traditions and the primarily functional orientation of the sending tradition."

after the latter's mission on earth as a relationship between separate beings; the Johannine Logos is a person, not simply a personification. The Fourth Evangelist thought in terms of personal preexistence; 1:1-3 and 1:18 have to be read in connection with 17:5 and 17:24.[33] Essential is an intimate relationship between the Son and the Father, characterized by love and shared "glory" (1:14), from before the foundation of the world to the Son's "glorification," his return to the presence of the Father.[34] This glory, essential to the relationship between this only Son and his Father, became visible during the Son's mission on earth (1:14; 2:11; 11:4, 40); he was the one who made the Father known. Although he himself may be called "god," he remains dependent on the Father. The one addressed by Thomas as "my Lord and my God" (20:28) is a few verses later referred to with the traditional designations "the Christ/Messiah, the Son of God" (v. 31) — to be interpreted, of course, in a typically Johannine fashion.[35]

The return of the Son to the Father ends the Son's mission on earth; as we have already noted, it is followed by the sending of the Spirit as (another) Paraclete to the community of believers (14:16; 15:26; 16:7). The Spirit will bring about a more intense and more complete understanding of Jesus' words and actions on behalf of the Father. Chapters 13–17 deal at great length with the Spirit-led life of the community of believers. After Jesus' resurrection and exaltation, the disciples live in a period that is, in fact, an intensified continuation of the Son's mission on earth. "Very truly, I tell you, the one who believes in me will also do the works that I do, and, in fact, will do greater works than these, because I am going to my Father. I will do whatever you ask in my name, so that the Father may be glorified in the Son. If in my name you ask me for anything, I will do it" (14:12-14).

In this respect there is a parallel between John and Paul, and with pre-Pauline Christianity after Easter. But what did the Johannine com-

---

33. On the use of *theos* (God) in 1:1-3, 18 (cf. 20:28), see Loader, *The Christology of the Fourth Gospel,* 157: "Within this stream (i.e., the Wisdom/Logos stream), at least in Philo *theos* had been transferred as a title to the logos without compromise of monotheism." Cf. the use of Ps. 82:6 in 10:31-39. See also W. A. Meeks, "Equal to God," esp. 312-16.

34. Hence 12:41, where we hear that Isaiah saw Jesus' glory and spoke about him (cf. Isa. 6:1).

35. So also Loader, *The Christology of the Fourth Gospel,* 78, 166. Compare also "Son of God" in 10:36 (the implications of which are explained in vv. 37-38) after the use of "god" in 10:33-35.

munity believe about what was yet to come? Johannine christology has clearly remained theocentric, but what about the eschatological framework of this christology?[36]

It is essential, I think, to note that John's eschatology, with its special emphasis on the present effects of the Son's mission to the world, is the corollary of his radical christology.[37] This is clear, for instance, in Jesus' discourse with the Jews in 5:17-30, which stresses the Son's unity with and dependence upon the Father: "Whatever the Father does, the Son does likewise" (5:19). This also applies to the giving of life and the passing of judgment. Hence Jesus may declare: "Very truly, I tell you, anyone who hears my word and believes him who sent me has eternal life, and does not come under judgment, but has passed from death to life" (5:24; cf. 3:16-21).

In the following verses (5:25-29) this is connected with the traditional conceptions of the final judgment and the resurrection of the dead. In Paul, too, the last judgment can be transferred to Jesus (2 Cor. 5:10), as can the giving of life at the resurrection (Phil. 3:21). For John these take place now (5:25: "the hour is coming and is now here, when the dead will hear the voice of the Son of God, and those who hear will live"), just as they will take place in the future, when all who are in their graves will hear his word (5:28-29). Dahl has persuasively argued that the injunction "do not be astonished at this" in v. 28 constitutes an appeal to traditional doctrine: anyone who believes in a future judgment and resurrection should not be surprised that the Son of God gives life and exercises judgment now.[38]

36. There is nothing on this problem in the publications mentioned in note 18, apart from some passing remarks in Barrett, "Christocentric or Theocentric?" and Hartman, "Johannine Jesus-Belief and Monotheism." Loader cannot find a proper place for future eschatological sayings in Johannine christology; see Loader, *The Christology of the Fourth Gospel,* 92, 204-5, 221-22, and 212: "They (i.e., the references to traditionally future eschatology) are now almost superfluous; for, since soteriology and eschatology necessarily follow christology, future hope for believers will be fulfilled when they join their Lord where he is (17:24); yet traditional motifs of eschatology persist."

37. See M. de Jonge, "The Radical Eschatology of the Fourth Gospel and the Eschatology of the Synoptics: Some Suggestions," in A. Denaux, ed., *John and the Synoptics* (BETL 101; Leuven: Leuven University Press and Peeters, 1991) 481-87; see also the chapter "Eschatology and Ethics in the Fourth Gospel" in de Jonge, *Jesus: Stranger from Heaven and Son of God,* 169-91.

38. See N. A. Dahl, " 'Do Not Wonder!' John 5:28-29 and Johannine Eschatology Once More," in Fortna and Gaventa, eds., *The Conversation Continues,* 322-36, esp. 326-30.

For Dahl the references to future events are not corrections (by a later redactor, for instance) of the sayings about the present life and judgment; the former support the latter, just as the latter do not correct but supplement the former. Dahl is quite right when he remarks: "In chapter 6 the repeated statement 'and I will raise him up on the last day' points to an eschatological verification of Jesus' promise to the believers whom the Father has given to the Son (6:39-40, 44, 54); on the last day those who reject Jesus and his words are to be judged by the word that he has spoken (12:48)."[39] The conversation between Jesus and Martha in 11:23-27 also takes future resurrection and judgment for granted. Jesus stipulates, however, that not only "those who believe in me, even though they die, will live," but also "everyone who lives and believes will never die" (vv. 25-26).[40]

In this view the Gospel of John does not neglect or deny traditional Christian expectations of a crowning eschatological event, but rather tries to convince fellow Christians that these expectations can only be fully believed when one accepts the radical, "high" christology of the Johannine community (forged in severe arguments and struggles with Pharisaic Judaism in the immediate past), and its emphasis on the present effects of the Son's mission on earth.

This view of Johannine eschatology presupposes (as Dahl points out in his essay) that the Fourth Gospel, as we have it, represents a rather advanced stage in Johannine theology and functions in a dialogue with other Christian groups. I agree, and I am also inclined to think that there will not have been much difference in time between the final redaction of the Gospel and the Epistles,[41] in which the emphasis on future eschatological events is rather pronounced (note, for instance, the Antichrist in 1 John 2:18; Christ's parousia in 2:28–3:3; the day of judgment in 4:17). It would be very strange indeed if there had been a stage in Johannine thinking in which future eschatology played no part at all — in contrast to earlier Christian thought and to later developments in Johannine circles.[42] The statements about God acting through

---

39. Ibid., 328. One may add here 3:36 (cf. 9:41); 6:27; 12:35.

40. The raising of Lazarus, now, reveals God's glory (v. 40), manifesting itself in the deed of the one sent by him (v. 42; cf. vv. 3, 14).

41. See de Jonge, *Jesus: Stranger from Heaven and Son of God*, 97-102 and 193-222, esp. 209-10.

42. As M. Hengel, *The Johannine Question*, 76, has put it: "Nowhere in earliest Christianity is there a completely 'present eschatology' without any future element: that

Jesus and the Spirit in the present presuppose and, in fact, require (to use Dahl's felicitous phrase once more) "eschatological verification."

As I have argued elsewhere, these statements also call for the termination of the tension characteristic of the community of believers.[43] In John 13–17, chapters which deal with the life of the disciples after Jesus' departure, indicative and imperative alternate; mutual love reigns but has to be maintained. The disciples experience the hatred of the world and have to be exhorted to remain faithful. The Son, at his return to the Father, has overcome the world (16:33; cf. 12:31; 16:11). In fact, the Father had placed all things in his hand, right from the beginning of his mission (3:35; 13:3; 17:2). There is no need for the disciples to fear the world, yet they lead a troubled life (16:2, 33). Will it ever end?

It will, as is said in 14:1-3 and 17:24-26, strategic passages in the farewell discourses. These texts do not refer, I think, to the combined fates of individual believers (who will find true life with their Lord when they follow him: 12:24-26; 13:33-36), but to the destination of the believing community as a whole when, at the end, it will be taken out of the world and be free from the tribulation inherent to life in the interim period. The believers are destined to see the glory of the Son which the Father has given him, because he loved him before the foundation of the world (17:24). This "high" christological statement is found in the Son's prayer to the Father in John 17; it is, therefore, eminently theocentric. It also refers back to the Prologue (1:1-18).

The Fourth Gospel concentrates on the destiny of the disciples (as does the First Epistle). They will form a community of Jews and non-Jews scattered over the world (10:16; 11:52; 12:32; 17:20). But God did send the Son to save the world; the world was able to see what God did through Jesus (14:31; 15:22-23), and when it watches the unity and love in the community of the disciples it will be able to believe that God has

---

is a quite modern theological invention." Alois Stimpfle, in his recent treatment of the eschatology of the Fourth Gospel, *Blinde Sehen: Die Eschatologie im traditionsgeschichtlichen Prozess des Johannesevangeliums* (BZNW 57; Berlin: de Gruyter, 1990), comes to the extraordinary conclusion that the Fourth Gospel situates eschatological decisions about life and death exclusively in the present. Future apocalyptic statements occur but are only meant to lead the noninitiated astray; only the elect are able to understand their true meaning. This theory carries to the extreme the often defended view of the Fourth Gospel as a book for insiders.

43. See de Jonge, "The Radical Eschatology of the Fourth Gospel."

indeed sent him (13:35; 17:21-23). The Johannine community is called to make clear to the outside world that true life consists in living in communion with the Son and the Father. It is also called "to worship the Father in spirit and truth"; God is spirit and seeks such worshippers (4:23-24); no doubt the worshipping community is intended to include all humanity. But nowhere are we told when and how God's salvation of the world through the Son will be realized. Chapter 17 ends, in verses 24-26, on a negative note, as far as this is concerned: "Righteous Father, the world has not known you, but I know you, and these know that you have sent me" (v. 24). At this point the Johannine writings do not present as complete a picture of the future as one would wish, yet Johannine Christianity must have reckoned with some form of realization of God's salvation affecting all humanity and his entire creation.

CHAPTER 10

The One God and Jesus

The chief characteristic of the message and faith of the followers of Jesus, expressed in the early Christian writings of the first century C.E., is "Jesus centricity." When the early Christians spoke about God, they had to speak about Jesus; and when they spoke about Jesus, they had to introduce God. "Theology" implied "christology," and "christology" implied "theology." Jesus' followers were Jews and believed in the one and only God who had revealed himself to Abraham, Isaac, and Jacob, to Moses, and to the prophets. He was the One who had said: "I am the LORD your God who brought you out of Egypt, out of the land of slavery. You must have no other gods besides me" (Exod. 20:2-3; cf. Deut. 5:6-7; 6:4-5). But they also believed that this God had revealed himself anew, and decisively, in the words and deeds of Jesus, whom he had raised from the dead and exalted to heavenly glory. They hailed the risen Jesus as the heavenly Lord who determined their lives and would appear again to realize God's sovereign rule on earth. In due course they also assigned to him other functions; a number of texts, for instance, emphasize his presence and mediation when God created the world (1 Cor. 8:6; Col. 1:15-17; John 1:1-3). There is a great variety in early Christian christology, which used many designations for Jesus and many different lines of thought in defining his past, present, and future role in God's involvement in human affairs — influenced by a great number of passages from the scriptures, read and interpreted with a view to Jesus.

Christology is, indeed, a specific feature of early (and later) Christian belief. But, as was argued in the previous chapter, "christology" formed part of "eschatology" (that is, the complex of ideas about *God's* intervention in the future) and remained, therefore, closely connected with "theology" proper. Jewish eschatological expectation took many forms, but it always centered around a decisive intervention by God. God might employ one or more intermediary or redeemer figures — a messiah-king, a prophet, a new priest, angels, or an archangel — or he might not. The essential element is the radical change, the beginning of a new era in which all resistance to God's sovereign rule will be broken. The early followers of Jesus focused a number of important aspects of this expectation in Jesus — hence the "Jesus centricity" of their eschatology, which did indeed develop into a "christology."

In the present chapter I shall argue that when early Christians spoke about the central role of Jesus in God's dealings with Israel and humanity, they did not in the least want to question or to jeopardize the sovereignty of the one God of Israel ("monotheism"). With regard to this central aspect of its faith, first-century Christianity remained within the Jewish context in which it originated.

Yet it cannot be denied that there are aspects of christology that may possibly have endangered the loyalty to the one God of Israel, and it is right to have a closer look at the passages in which these aspects come to the fore. We shall have to ask whether similar ways of expression are found in contemporary ancient Judaism, and whether those were felt to be compatible with Jewish monotheism. Now there has been much debate lately on the question whether monotheism is the right term to characterize Jewish belief in the God of Israel in this period.[1] Larry Hurtado has, however, rightly made a distinction between "the variety and flexibility in ancient Jewish monotheistic tradition, especially the ability to accommodate 'divine' figures in addition to the God of Israel in the belief structure and religious outlook" and "scruples about worship and prayer to figures

---

1. See L. W. Hurtado, "What Do We Mean by 'First-Century Jewish Monotheism'?" in E. Lovering, ed., *SBL 1993 Seminar Papers* (Atlanta: Scholars Press, 1993), 348-68; idem, *One God, One Lord: Early Christian Devotion and Ancient Jewish Monotheism* (Philadelphia: Fortress, 1988); C. Rowland, *The Open Heaven: A Study of Apocalyptic in Judaism and Early Christianity* (London: SPCK, 1982), especially 94-113; A. P. Hayman, "Monotheism — A Misused Word in Jewish Studies?" *JJS* 42 (1991) 1-15; M. Barker, *The Great Angel: A Study of Israel's Second God* (London: SPCK, 1992); and J. D. G. Dunn, *The Partings of the Ways between Christianity and Judaism and Their Significance for the Character of Christianity* (London: SCM; Philadelphia: Trinity Press International, 1991), especially Chapters 9–11, pp. 163-229.

other than God."[2] In this essay we will pay special attention to the question whether, and to what extent, ideas about the "divine" status and function of the exalted, heavenly Jesus led to devotion comparable to the worship due to the God of Israel.

After the previous chapters we can be brief about the views of Jesus and his followers during his lifetime, about the ideas of our oldest witness, Paul, and about the christology presupposed in formulas used by Paul. Next, some texts and notions in Matthew, Hebrews, and Revelation will be considered. The last section will be devoted to the Fourth Gospel, a key witness to the issue with which we are concerned.

Jesus and Paul

In Chapter 3 we found that there is a broad consensus among scholars that Jesus announced and even claimed to inaugurate the coming of God's sovereign rule on earth. The kingdom of God was at hand. Jesus announced it and called people to repentance (Mark 1:15; cf. Luke 10:9, par. Matt. 10:7). Hence his radical ethic and the authority with which he approached people in the name of God. At the same time, he assured his hearers: "But if it is by the finger of God that I drive out the demons, then be sure the kingdom of God has already come upon you" (Luke 11:20, par. Matt. 12:28). Hence his concern for the sick, the sinners, the poor, and the oppressed. In the Lord's Prayer the concentration on God's rule is connected with trust in God as a Father (Luke 11:2, par. Matt. 6:9-10; cf. Gal. 4:4-7; Rom. 8:14-17).

Jesus' conviction that he announced and inaugurated God's kingdom (soon to be fully realized on earth) implies a christology; but this is a theocentric christology, in an eschatological setting. Whether he himself used the christological "titles" Messiah or Son of God, or whether these were connected with him by others during his lifetime, is of minor importance for our present investigation, as became clear in Chapter 8. It is evident that Jesus was convinced that he was called to his mission by God, and that he acted and spoke from an intimate relationship with the One whom he called his Father. It is possible and

2. Hurtado, "What Do We Mean by 'First-Century Jewish Monotheism'?" 355 and 363, going back to the central thesis of his *One God, One Lord.*

even likely that he regarded himself as Messiah, but the Messiah is essentially an agent of God, acting on God's behalf at a crucial moment. With regard to the designation "Son of God," a term used in many different ways in contemporary Judaism, the situation is not very much different. We cannot be certain whether he called himself "Son of God," but he certainly spoke and acted as the Son authorized by the Father to be his representative at a supreme moment in history.

It is very difficult to reach certainty about Jesus' use of the term "Son of Man" (Chapter 7). The term must be regarded as a clear characteristic of Jesus' speech, and we have argued that Jesus used it in connection with Dan. 7:13, where "one like a son of man" receives dominion, glory, and kingship that are to last for ever. This will have entailed for him his vindication as messenger and inaugurator of the kingdom, despite the opposition he faced and the real prospect of a violent death. In the interpretation of the vision of Daniel 7, the "one like a son of man" is taken as the representative of the persecuted "people of the saints of the Most High" (Dan. 7:18, 21-22, 25, 27). Use of the imagery of this vision fits in with Jesus' "theocentric christology." He may well have expected to appear as Son of Man in glory when God's sovereign rule would become fully manifest in the entire creation.

It is clear that Dan. 7:13 has influenced the Christian expectation of Jesus' coming (back) to earth "with the clouds of heaven" (so Mark 13:26; 14:62) as ruler and judge and introducing the coming of God's kingdom in power (Mark 8:38–9:1). The expectation of a future coming of the Son of Man is essential for Mark as well as for Q (Luke 12:8-9, par. Matt. 10:32-33; Luke 12:40, par. Matt. 24:44; Luke 17:22, 24, 26, 30, par. Matt. 24:27, 37, 39). Here again the emphasis is on the fact that the Son of Man acts as representative of God.

With regard to the ideas of Paul, we may again rely on what we have found above, particularly in Chapters 2 and 9. In his letters many of the formulaic statements expressing early Christian beliefs are concerned with the meaning of Jesus' death and resurrection. The emphasis is on the resurrection as demonstration of the fact that the one who died on the cross had indeed been a righteous man, now declared righteous by God and sharing in God's glory. As parallels, we may point to Jewish texts about righteous suffering servants and martyrs. The insulted and tortured righteous man of Wisd. 2:12-20, who is God's servant and calls God his Father, turns out to be counted among the sons of God and to have received a place of his own among the saints

(5:1-7). The seven martyrs and their mother of 2 Maccabees 7 expect a resurrection to a new and everlasting life.[3]

A number of early resurrection formulas emphasize God's activity in raising Jesus from the dead (Rom. 4:24; 8:11; 10:9; 1 Cor. 6:14; 15:15; 2 Cor. 4:14; Gal. 1:1; 1 Thess. 1:10). Paul connects the resurrection of Jesus with the future resurrection of those who believe in him (1 Thess. 4:13-18; 1 Cor. 15:22-28). For Paul, and for early Christianity as a whole, God's vindication of Jesus shows that Jesus' message concerning God's sovereign rule and final salvation remains reliable and valid.

Jesus' mission, vindicated by his resurrection, marks a decisive step in the eschatological process. Therefore Jesus is acknowledged as Lord (1 Cor. 12:3), whose coming in power is eagerly awaited (*Maranatha*, 1 Cor. 16:22; cf. 1 Cor. 11:26; Phil. 3:20). Thus, in 2 Cor. 5:10 Christ is portrayed as sitting in the judgment seat, and in Phil. 3:20-21 the Lord Jesus Christ is expected to transfigure our humble bodies and give them a form like that of his glorious body.[4]

Believing in the resurrection of Jesus and acknowledging him as Lord are directly linked in Rom. 10:9: "if you confess with your lips that Jesus is Lord and believe in your heart that God raised him from the dead, you will be saved" (cf. v. 13). Romans 8:34 speaks about "Christ Jesus, who died, who was raised, who is at the right hand of God" and who is therefore able to intercede for believers with God. This verse alludes to Ps. 110:1, one of the most quoted passages from the Old Testament in the writings of the New Testament. God the LORD himself had exalted Jesus to lordship (so explicitly Acts 2:34-35; cf. Mark 12:36 and parallels; 14:62 and parallels). At the same time, 1 Cor. 15:25-28 (where not only Ps. 110:1 but also Ps. 8:7 is referred to) makes clear that at the end God will have the final say: "When all things are subjected to him, then the Son himself will also be subjected to the One who put all things in subjection under him, so that God may be all in all" (v. 28).

For followers of the resurrected Jesus, to confess him as Lord, to acclaim him, and to call for his coming in power (no doubt in the setting

---

3. See pp. 18-30 above. Hurtado, *One God, One Lord*, devotes his Chapter 3 to "Exalted Patriarchs as Divine Agents" (51-65). The material he assembles is important for a better understanding of early christology, but it is not directly concerned with resurrection.

4. See also L. J. Kreitzer, *Jesus and God in Paul's Eschatology* (JSNTSup19; Sheffield: Sheffield Academic Press, 1987).

of worship) clearly do not endanger the worship of the one God of Israel. This is also evident in the much discussed hymn preserved in Phil. 2:6-11, at the end of which God is said to have "highly exalted" Jesus and to have given him "the name above every name" (v. 9). The entire creation will confess that "Jesus Christ is Lord" (vv. 10-11), as predicted in Isa. 45:22-23, where all worship is centered on the One who says, "For I am God, and there is no other." Paul, and the composers of the hymn before him, saw no contradiction here; for them everyone confessing "Jesus Christ is Lord" did so "to the glory of God the Father" (Phil. 2:11). God was the initiator of all that Jesus as his eschatological agent had been called to perform and to represent.[5]

When early Christians like Paul proclaimed the message concerning Jesus Christ, they had to remind their non-Jewish hearers that they had to turn "to God from idols, to serve a living and true God" before they could put their hope in "his Son from heaven, whom he raised from the dead — Jesus, who rescues us from the wrath that is coming" (1 Thess. 1:9-10; cf. Acts 14:15-17; 17:24-31). So also 1 Cor. 8:6, "yet for us there is one God, the Father, from whom are all things and for whom we exist," echoes (among other things) the fundamental Jewish conviction expressed in the *Shema' Yisrael* in Deut. 6:4 and many other passages in the Old Testament. Yet the formula continues in the same breath "and one Lord, Jesus Christ, through whom are all things and through whom we exist." As in Col. 1:15-20, Jesus Christ is mentioned as the agent, the mediator, of creation as well as the agent of redemption. This implies a central role for him not only in the present and in the future, but also in the very beginning. He is thought to have been with God the creator and to have played a role at the creation. As has often been noted, Paul here identifies Jesus the Lord with divine Wisdom (see, e.g., Prov. 8:22-31; Sir. 24:1-12; Wisd. 7:26; 8:4-6; 9:1-4), a figure that played a key role in mythological reflection on God's initiative in creating the universe and on his interaction with humanity.[6] Again, this way of

---

5. God and Jesus Christ the Lord are mentioned together in the salutation formulas in the beginning of Paul's letters; see, e.g., Rom. 1:7, "Grace to you and peace from God our Father and the Lord Jesus Christ."

6. See, for instance, M. de Jonge, *Christology in Context: The Earliest Christian Response to Jesus* (Philadelphia: Westminster, 1988) 194-99; Hurtado, *One God, One Lord*, Chapter 2, "Personified Divine Attributes as Divine Agents" (41-44; he includes a section on the *logos* in Philo); Dunn, *The Partings of the Ways*, 195-201 (going back to earlier publications).

speaking about an associate of God does not seem in any way to have been perceived as a threat to the worship of the one, true God, neither in earlier and contemporary Jewish literature, nor in Christian texts (besides 1 Cor. 8:6 and Col. 1:15-20, see particularly John 1:1-3, which uses the term *logos*).

In addition to the title "Lord," however, was "God" also used in connection with Jesus? This does not seem to be the case in Rom. 9:5, a doxology centering on God "supreme above all" (REB). The application to Jesus may be made in the deutero-Pauline letter to Titus, which speaks of "our hope when the splendor of our God and Savior Christ Jesus will appear" (2:13). The same author, however, also describes Jesus as the one in whom "the kindness and generosity of God our Savior dawned upon the world" (Tit. 3:4). God and Jesus are united in one saving action.[7]

Matthew, Hebrews, and Revelation

The Gospel of Matthew has to be mentioned briefly because of its special form of theocentric christology.[8] In 1:23 Jesus is identified with the "Emmanuel" predicted in Isa. 7:14. This name is explicitly translated as "God with us." At the very end of the book, the theme returns in the promise of the risen Jesus in 28:20, "I am with you always to the end of the age"; in fact, all authority in heaven and on earth has been given to him, and his disciples have to baptize "in the name of the Father and of the Son and of the Holy Spirit" (vv. 19-20). Also worth mentioning here is Matt. 18:20: "where two or three are gathered in my name, I am there among them."[9]

The Epistle to the Hebrews emphasizes the exaltation of Jesus in a special way. God's revelation by the Son forms the climax of his dealings through the prophets (1:1-2). He is "the heir of all things," "the

---

7. Compare the very late text 2 Pet. 1:1, which has the expression "the righteousness of our God and Savior Jesus Christ." See further below on the Gospel of John.

8. See Dunn, *The Partings of the Ways*, 213-15.

9. Another particular Matthean feature is the identification of Jesus with Wisdom in Matt. 11:19 (cf. 11:2); 11:28-30; 23:34 (and vv. 37-39). One should compare here the parallels in Luke (probably representing Q).

radiance of God's glory," the mediator at creation, and the one who "sustains all things by the word of his power" (vv. 2-3). The term "Son" is not only connected with Wisdom christology but is also explained by means of Ps. 110:1: "When he had made purification for sins, he sat down at the right hand of the Majesty on high" (v. 3). The following verses (vv. 5-14) stress that the Son is superior to all angels and spirits. Even Ps. 45:7-8, taken to mention a royal figure addressed as God ("O God, your God has anointed you with the oil of gladness above your fellows") is applied to Jesus.

Psalm 110:1 plays an important role in Hebrews (1:3, 13; 8:1; 10:12; 12:2; cf. Ps. 8:5-7 in 2:6-8). The Son of God is more powerful than all his adversaries, who one day will be annihilated forever. Hence he is a trustworthy helper for those who put their trust in him. This is highlighted by calling him "high priest." Probably already before Hebrews Jesus was regarded as such (2:17; 3:1; 4:15; 5:5-10; cf. Rom. 8:34), but the author of the epistle develops this christology in a special way by connecting verse 1 of the psalm with verse 4 (5:6, 10; 6:20; chapter 7) and combining the notion of eternal priesthood with that of Christ as sacrifice (see esp. chapters 8–10). Elsewhere the emphasis is not only on the effects of Jesus' death but also on the fact that he was perfected in suffering in order to become an effective helper for those related to him (2:9-18; 4:14-16; 5:5-10).

In Revelation, many scholars have drawn attention to the opening vision in 1:12-16.[10] There "one like a son of man" (Dan. 7:13) appears with a head and hair "as white wool, white as snow" (cf. the description of the Ancient of Days in Dan. 7:9). As often in the Apocalypse, the imagery is influenced by numerous other Old Testament passages as well. The most intriguing phenomenon is the combination of elements taken from Dan. 7:9 and 7:13 to describe a single figure. In Rev. 1:17-18 this figure reveals himself as Jesus ("I was dead, and see, I am alive for ever"); again divine epithets are used to describe him ("the first and the last" — Isa. 44:6; 48:12; Rev. 1:8; 2:8; 21:6; 22:13 — "the living one"). Parallels to these portrayals of Jesus are found in descriptions of glorious angelic figures who act as principal agents on behalf of God — a notion finally going back to the Old Testament figure of "the angel of the Lord," who represents God himself, and who (in practice)

10. See Rowland, *The Open Heaven;* Hurtado, *One God, One Lord,* 71-92; Dunn, *The Partings of the Ways,* 215-20.

was identified with him in contacts with human beings (see, e.g., Exodus 3; Judges 13).[11]

Much discussion has been devoted to the question whether in Revelation, and already in Jewish texts, we should speak of a process of "bifurcation" of God (so Christopher Rowland) or rather of an incipient "binitarianism" (so Larry Hurtado and James Dunn). Perhaps we should allow for a great deal of flexibility in apocalyptic imagery and terminology, and regard neither term as quite appropriate. God and the exalted Jesus as his one and only eschatological agent have become inseparable. On the heavenly worship of God on his throne in Revelation 4 (no doubt exemplary for worship on earth) follows the worship of God and the Lamb in chapter 5. They are praised together: "To the one seated on the throne and the Lamb be blessing and honor and glory and might for ever and ever!" (5:13; cf. 7:10). God on his heavenly throne remains the center of all worship (7:11-17), and adoration of the Lamb in no way endangers or diminishes the worship due to him. The Lamb is pictured in the immediate presence of God (5:6-7; 7:9), even at the center of the throne (7:17). In the vision of the heavenly Jerusalem, there is only one throne of God and the Lamb (22:1, 3; cf. 3:21).[12] The danger against which the readers are warned is worship of the Dragon and the Beast (chapter 13; 14:9-12; 19:20-21); they should fear God and give him glory (14:7). At the same time, the seer is told not to worship the angel who acts as intermediary for his visions (19:10; 22:8-9). The exalted Jesus Christ is worshipped together with God and is superior to any angel.

---

11. See, for instance, Michael in Dan. 12:1 and in 1QM; Melchizedek in 11QMelch (called "god"); the unnamed angel in *Jos. As.* 14:9. In other (later) texts we meet Eremiel (*Apoc. Zeph.* 6:11-15) and Iaoel (*Apocalypse of Abraham* 10–11; cf. Exod. 23:20-21).

12. There is an interesting parallel in the *Similitudes of Enoch*, where not only will God ("the Head of Days," "the Lord of Spirits") deliver judgment on his throne (47:3; 62:2,3) but "the Chosen One"/"the Son of Man" will be seated on the throne of his glory (45:3; 51:3; 55:4; 61:8; 69:27, 29) to judge on God's behalf. As J. Tromp pointed out to me, in 48:5 people worshipping the Son of Man praise the name of the Lord of Spirits (cf. 62:9-10).

The Fourth Gospel

The Fourth Gospel presupposes a radical break between the synagogue and its leaders and the Johannine community (9:22, 34; 16:2; cf. 12:42). This separation must have been a traumatic experience leading to much reflection and discussion within the Johannine community and, in particular, to a refinement and radicalization of the community's view of Jesus' relationship to God and his mission on earth. In 9:22 we hear: "For the Jews had already agreed that anyone who confessed Jesus to be the Messiah would be put out of the synagogue." The context (see especially 9:35-38) shows that the particular Johannine view of Jesus as the Messiah, Son of God, and Son of Man was involved (see John 20:31; cf. 10:24-30; 11:27). In a long series of exchanges that Jesus has with interested outsiders and followers, as well as in his debates with critical Jewish opponents, a number of particular Johannine aspects of the relationship between God and Jesus, the Father and the Son, are developed and brought out clearly.

In the altercations with "the Jews," the reproach of the opponents that Jesus made himself (Son of) God stands out clearly. In 5:18 the Jews are portrayed as seeking to kill Jesus (cf. 7:1, 19, 25, 30; 8:37, 40, 59; 10:31, 33; 11:8) "because he was not only breaking the Sabbath, but was also calling God his own father, *making himself equal to God.*" This charge is followed in 10:33 by the remark, "It is not for a good work that we are going to stone you, but for blasphemy, because you, though a human being, *are making yourself God*" (cf. v. 36). Finally, in 19:7 the Jews declare: "We have a law, and according to that law he ought to die, *because he has made himself Son of God.*"

In order to safeguard the truth revealed in Jesus and the experience of new life in communion with the exalted Christ and the Spirit sent by him, the Johannine community stressed, all along, the unique and intimate connection between Jesus and God. This clearly was regarded by their Jewish opponents as a threat to, if not a straightforward denial of, the uniqueness of the God of Israel. In this conflict the Johannine Christians continued to emphasize that it was by no means human arrogance that made Jesus say, "My Father is still working, and I am working" (5:17) or claim, "I have shown you many good works from the Father" (10:32). Indeed, "the Son can do nothing on his own, but only what he sees the Father doing; for whatever he does, the Son does likewise" (5:19). This even includes raising the dead and giving life, as well as pronouncing judgment (5:20-22), "so that all may honor the Son just as they honor the Father" (5:23). Jesus, a human being, has not usurped the prerogatives of the one and only God; it is God himself who has entrusted him with a singular mission on earth. All that Jesus says and does comes from God.

The Fourth Gospel has developed the christology of mission already found in Gal. 4:4-7; Rom. 8:3-4; and Mark 12:1-9 in great detail, in order to defend the uniqueness of Jesus' words and works as well as to highlight the Son's dependence on the Father and his complete obedience to him. Johannine christology, with all its statements about Jesus' unity with God, remains theocentric. As has often been noted, the phrase "he (or: the Father) who has sent me (him)" is in this Gospel the most frequent expression found in connection with Jesus, alongside "whom the Father has sent." In all cases an active form of the verb is used, so that the emphasis is placed on the sending activity of God, in which the unity of speech, will, and action between God and Jesus — Father and Son — is grounded. The Son does nothing "on his own" (5:19, 30; 7:17, 28; 8:28, 42; 12:49; 14:10). He does God's will (4:34; 5:30; 6:38-40), for he has to perform/complete God's work (4:34; 5:36; 10:37-38; 14:12; 17:4). His works are the works of the Father, and the Father works through him (14:10).

The perfect unity between the Father and the Son is expressed in various ways. The word "love" is used many times (e.g., in 3:35; 5:20; 10:17). The Father has not only sent the Son on his mission but maintains contact with him (5:19-20, 30; 8:16, 29; 16:32). In 10:30 Jesus uses the expression "I and the Father are one" in order to underline that whatever he does is done by the Father. A bit later the language of mutual indwelling is used: "believe that the Father is in me and I am in the Father" (10:38; cf. 17:21-23). This may be connected with the "I am" sayings attributed to Jesus. Those with a predicate ("I am the bread of life," etc.) express that Jesus grants true life on behalf of God, and that the gift and the Giver are identical. Where "I am" is used without a predicate (8:24, 28, 58; 13:19), it functions as a revelation formula comparable to those found in Deutero Isaiah (e.g., Isa. 43:10). Jesus reveals himself in the way God reveals himself: "I have made your name known to those whom you gave me from the world," says Jesus to God in 17:5 (cf. v. 26; 12:28).

The Logos christology in the Prologue (1:1-18), which is directly related to the Wisdom christology found in 1 Cor. 8:6 (and elsewhere), underscores the close relationship, from the very beginning, between God and the Word, which appeared among men in the person of Jesus. The Logos was the source of light and life (1:4-5, 7-9). When this Logos dwelt among men, believers saw "his glory, the glory as of the Father's only son" (1:14; cf. 2:11; 11:4, 40; 12:41). True knowledge of God comes through him. "Nobody has ever seen God (cf. 5:37; 6:46; 14:9); the only Son, (himself) God, who is at the bosom of the Father, he has made him known" (1:18). In this text-critically difficult verse, the only Son is probably called *theos*, as is the Logos in v. 1. We may compare Thomas's confession, "My Lord and my God" at the end of the Gospel (20:28). The use of *theos* here singles out the Logos/Son as the supreme and unique intermediary of God's self-revelation before, during, and after Jesus' mission on earth.[13] This attempt at expressing the uniqueness of Jesus' mission also aims at safeguarding theocentricity. The initiative is with God, from the very beginning to the very end.

The great effort spent in making clear that Jesus' unique position in God's dealings with humanity and his close relationship as Son to the Father in no way led to his deification or to an infringement on monotheism as understood by the Jews, shows that the Johannine community took the criticism of its Jewish opponents seriously. It is not surprising that outsiders interpreted as dangerous and even blasphemous the insistence of the Johannine community on the close unity between the exalted Son and the Father (as expressed in 1:18; 10:30, 38; 17:21-23), which led to honoring the Son in the same way as the Father (5:23; cf. 20:28), as well as on the intimate relationship of believers with Father and Son (14:20, 23; 17:21-23).[14] Hence the emphasis of the Gospel on descent before ascent (3:13) and the elaboration of the mission christology in order to highlight God's initiative. The

13. On the use of *theos* in connection with men in the Greek world, see W. A. Meeks, "Equal to God," in R. T. Fortna and B. R. Gaventa, eds., *The Conversation Continues: Studies in Paul and John in Honor of J. Louis Martyn* (Nashville: Abingdon, 1990) 309-21, especially 312-14. Philo had no difficulties in calling the Logos *theos;* see Hurtado, *One God, One Lord,* 44-48. See also John 10:31-39, with a reference to Ps. 82:6, a psalm also used in 11QMelch, where Melchizedek is described as *'ĕlōhîm.*

14. The attitude of the Jewish critics of the Johannine views has been compared to the condemnation of the "two powers heresy" by second-century rabbis, criticizing (among others) some types of apocalyptic and early merkabah mysticism. See, for instance, Dunn, *The Partings of the Ways,* 223-24; and A. F. Segal, *Two Powers in Heaven: Early Rabbinic Reports about Christianity and Gnosticism* (SJLA 25; Leiden: Brill, 1977).

God of Abraham, Isaac, Jacob, and Moses had himself assigned this special position to Jesus. To accept this and to put one's trust in Jesus as the Messiah, the Son of God, is the way to eternal life.

Summing Up

Let us briefly look back on the way we have traveled. To begin with, we would know very little about Jesus if there had not been a group of followers who, after his death on the cross, stuck together and continued to believe in his message. It is important to stress that they *continued* to believe in him, and that they believed in him as *God's final envoy*. In its earliest stages, the Christian message about Jesus (found in traditional elements in the letters of Paul, in Q, and in Mark) is concerned with the meaning of his death and resurrection; it presupposes that in Jesus God had brought a decisive and definitive turn in the history of Israel and of the entire world. This conviction must have been present before the first Easter. Already during Jesus' lifetime his disciples must have believed that as a prophet, teacher, and exorcist he was the herald and inaugurator of God's reign on earth — probably because their master was convinced he was sent by God to perform that task.

An examination of the many sayings of Jesus about the kingdom of God recorded in the Gospels (particularly those in Q and Mark) led to the conclusion that here, indeed, the core of Jesus' teaching is found. The emphasis falls on the complete breakthrough of the kingdom in the near future, bringing with it a definitive change in the world's affairs. It is all the more eagerly awaited because of the manifestation of God's rule in Jesus' words and actions. A survey of contemporary Jewish ideas about the kingdom of God has helped us see more clearly the particular features of the expectations concerning the future in Jesus' message and in that of his followers. The element of the dynamic presence of God's rule seems to be attested nowhere else.

The next question was how Jesus' message about the kingdom of God was related to his view of his suffering, death, and vindication by God. For early Christianity it was essential to believe that God had vindicated Jesus and his message — hence the many ways in which the implications of the resurrection, for believers and nonbelievers, are spelled out in our sources. The same is true of the many interpretations of the meaning of Jesus' death. Even if one concentrates on the earliest stages of the message concerning Jesus' resurrection and death, it is difficult to make out what Jesus believed himself. He may have interpreted his fate as that of God's final envoy to Israel, and he may have seen himself as an obedient servant of God who would be vindicated. It is difficult to say with certainty whether he regarded his death as that of a martyr dying for others.

An analysis of Mark 14:25, in connection with other sayings about the future of God's kingdom, brought to light that this logion, which speaks about Jesus' participation in the joy of the kingdom, presupposes the vindication of Jesus' message and his person by God after death. It does not, however, assign to him a central role in the final breakthrough of God's sovereign rule on earth, and it does not mention his parousia. The expectation of Jesus' parousia — his return from heaven as judge and king — is of central importance in early Christianity. It is found in Paul's letters, in Mark, and in Q, as well as in further sayings found in Matthew and Luke. In the Gospels the title "Son of Man" is often connected with this concept. In all likelihood, Jesus himself did not expect to return as Son of Man after a period of time, however short. Inspired by Daniel 7, he expected his vindication as messenger of the kingdom to take place, during his suffering in life or at his death, in the form of his appearance as the Son of Man at the moment when God would intervene to establish his sovereign rule on earth once and for all. After his death his followers realized that Jesus' personal vindication, now viewed as resurrection, and the complete breakthrough of the kingdom of God, accompanied by Jesus' return from heaven, were two separate events — one now in the past, the other awaited in the future.

Jesus' own "christology" was implicit rather than explicit. He believed himself to have been sent as God's final envoy, as the inaugurator of God's rule on earth, which would later be realized completely in the entire creation. Everything centered around the sovereignty and fatherhood of God. Jesus' christology was "theocentric" from beginning to end. This would remain so even if it could be proven beyond doubt that he called himself explicitly "the Messiah" or "the Son of God." As God's final envoy Jesus saw himself as standing in a unique relationship to God, whom he addressed as Father. It is probable that he regarded himself as Messiah and Son of David, inspired and empowered by the Spirit. The use of these titles, however, does not in any way impinge on the theocentricity of Jesus' christology.

This is true not only of how Jesus viewed his relationship to God and his mission, but also of how his immediate disciples and the next generation of followers viewed him. Christology is a form of eschatology. Jewish eschatological expectation took many forms, but it always centered around the awaited decisive intervention by God — who might or might not employ human or angelic intermediaries. Jesus' expectation was thoroughly Jewish in this respect, notwithstanding his conviction that he himself was called upon to play a crucial role in the process. The same is also true of the expectations of his followers after his death, when, in the light of God's vindication of Jesus in the resurrection, they emphasized Jesus' very special and intimate relationship to God and the central part he was expected to play in the forthcoming events. Even the Johannine Christians, whose views are represented in the Fourth Gospel, had a theocentric christology that did not intend to endanger the loyalty to the one God of Israel.

Select Bibliography

Earlier publications by the author used in the preparation of this volume:

"The Christological Significance of Jesus' Preaching of the Kingdom of God." In *The Future of Christology: Essays in Honor of Leander E. Keck*, edited by Abraham J. Malherbe and Wayne A. Meeks, 1-17. Minneapolis: Fortress, 1993. Used in several chapters.

"Christology and Theology in the Context of Early Christian Eschatology Particularly in the Fourth Gospel." In *The Four Gospels 1992: Festschrift Frans Neirynck*, edited by F. Van Segbroeck et al., 1835-53. BETL 100. Leuven: University Press and Peeters, 1992. Used in Chapter 9.

Jesus' Message about the Kingdom of God in the Light of Contemporary Ideas. The Ethel M. Wood Lecture, 1991. London: University of London, 1991. Used in Chapters 3 and 4.

"Jesus' Rôle in the Final Breakthrough of God's Kingdom." In *Geschichte — Tradition — Reflexion: Festschrift für Martin Hengel zum 70. Geburtstag*, edited by Hubert Cancik, Hermann Lichtenberger, and Peter Schäfer, vol. 3, 265-86. Tübingen: Mohr Siebeck, 1996. Used in Chapters 6 and 7.

Jesus, The Servant-Messiah. New Haven: Yale University Press, 1991. Used in parts of Chapters 1 and 8, and in Chapter 2.

"Mark 14:25 among Jesus' Words about the Kingdom of God." In *Sayings of Jesus, Canonical and Non-Canonical: Essays in Honour of Tjitze Baarda*, edited by William L. Petersen, Johan S. Vos, and Henk J. de Jonge, 123-35. NovTSup 89. Leiden: Brill, 1997. Used in Chapter 5.

"Monotheism and Christology." In *Early Christian Thought in Its Jewish Context*, edited by John Barclay and John Sweet, 225-37. Cambridge: Cambridge University Press, 1995. Used in Chapter 10.

Often reference is made to the author's study:

Christology in Context: The Earliest Christian Response to Jesus. Philadelphia: Westminster, 1988.

Other collections of essays on christology by the author:

Jesus: Inspiring and Disturbing Presence. Translated by John E. Steely. Nashville: Abingdon, 1974.
Jesus: Stranger from Heaven and Son of God. SBLSBS 11. Missoula, Mont.: Scholars Press, 1977.
Jewish Eschatology, Early Christian Christology, and the Testaments of the Twelve Patriarchs: Collected Essays. Edited by Henk J. de Jonge. NovTSup 63. Leiden: Brill, 1991.

Direct "sparring partners" — the contributors to the following volumes:

Boer, Martinus C. de, ed. *From Jesus to John: Essays on Jesus and New Testament Christology in Honour of Marinus de Jonge.* JSNTSup 84. Sheffield: Sheffield Academic Press, 1993.
Gennep, F. O. van, et al. *Waarlijk Opgestaan! Een discussie over de opstanding van Jezus Christus.* 2d ed. Baarn: Ten Have, 1994.
Heering, J. P., et al., eds. *Jezus' visie op Zichzelf: In discussie met de Jonge's christologie.* Nijkerk: Callenbach, 1991.
Jonge, Henk J. de, and B. W. J. de Ruyter, eds. *Totdat hij komt: Een discussie over de wederkomst van Jezus Christus.* Baarn: Ten Have, 1995.

And in particular also:

Jonge, Henk J. de. "Ontstaan en ontwikkeling van het geloof in Jezus' opstanding." In *Waarlijk opgestaan! Een discussie over de opstanding van Jezus Christus,* by F. O. van Gennep et al., 31-50. 2d ed. Baarn: Ten Have, 1994.
———. "De opstanding van Jezus: De joodse traditie achter een christelijke belijdenis." In *Jodendom en vroeg christendom: Continuïteit en discontinuïteit,* by Tjitze Baarda et al., 47-61. Kampen: Kok, 1991.
———. "Visionaire ervaring en de historische oorsprong van het christendom." Inaugural Lecture, University of Leiden, January 17, 1992.
Henten, Jan W. van. *The Maccabean Martyrs as Saviours of the Jewish People: A Study of 2 and 4 Maccabees.* JSJSup 57. Leiden: Brill.
Holleman, Joost. *Resurrection and Parousia: A Traditio-Historical Study of Paul's Eschatology in 1 Corinthians 15.* NovTSup 84. Leiden: Brill, 1996.

Other important studies:

Barrett, C. K. *Jesus and the Gospel Tradition.* London: SPCK, 1967.

Beasley-Murray, G. R. *Jesus and the Kingdom of God.* Grand Rapids: Eerdmans; Exeter: Paternoster, 1986.

Bühner, Jan-A. *Der Gesandte und sein Weg im 4. Evangelium.* WUNT 2/2. Tübingen: Mohr Siebeck, 1977.

Camponovo, Odo. *Königtum, Königsherrschaft und Reich Gottes in den frühjüdischen Schriften.* OBO 58. Freiburg: Universitätsverlag; Göttingen: Vandenhoeck & Ruprecht, 1984.

Chilton, Bruce. *Pure Kingdom: Jesus' Vision of God.* Grand Rapids: Eerdmans, 1996.

Collins, John J. *The Scepter and the Star: The Messiahs of the Dead Sea Scrolls and Other Ancient Literature.* New York: Doubleday, 1995.

Dahl, Nils A. *Jesus the Christ: The Historical Origins of Christological Doctrine.* Edited by Donald H. Juel. Minneapolis: Fortress, 1991.

Delling, Gerhard. *Studien zum Neuen Testament und zum hellenistischen Judentum: Gesammelte Aufsätze 1950-1968.* Edited by F. Hahn, T. Holtz, and N. Walter. Göttingen: Vandenhoeck & Ruprecht, 1979.

Dunn, James D. G. *Christology in the Making: A New Testament Inquiry into the Origin of the Doctrine of the Incarnation.* Philadelphia: Westminster, 1980.

————. *The Partings of the Ways between Christianity and Judaism and Their Significance for the Character of Christianity.* London: SCM; Philadelphia: Trinity Press International, 1991.

Hahn, Ferdinand. "Methodische Überlegungen zur Rückfrage nach Jesus." In *Rückfrage nach Jesus: Zur Methodik und Bedeutung der Rückfrage nach dem historischen Jesus,* edited by Karl Kertelge, 11-77. QD 63. Freiburg: Herder, 1974.

Hengel, Martin. *The Atonement: The Origins of the Doctrine in the New Testament.* London: SCM, 1981.

————. *Between Jesus and Paul: Studies in the Earliest History of Christianity.* London: SCM, 1983.

————. *The Son of God.* Philadelphia: Fortress; London: SCM, 1976.

————. *Studies in Early Christology.* Edinburgh: Clark, 1995.

Hengel, Martin, and Anna Maria Schwemer, eds. *Königsherrschaft und himmlischer Kult im Judentum und in der hellenistischen Welt.* WUNT 55. Tübingen: Mohr Siebeck, 1991.

Hooker, Morna D. *Jesus and the Servant: The Influence of the Servant Concept of Deutero-Isaiah in the New Testament.* London: SPCK, 1959.

————. *The Son of Man in Mark.* London: SPCK, 1967.

Horsley, Richard A., and John S. Hanson. *Bandits, Prophets, and Messiahs: Popular Movements in the Time of Jesus.* 2d ed. New York: Harper and Row, 1988.

Hurtado, Larry W. *One God, One Lord: Early Christian Devotion and Ancient Jewish Monotheism.* Philadelphia: Fortress, 1988.

Keck, Leander E. *A Future for the Historical Jesus: The Place of Jesus in Preaching and Theology.* Nashville: Abingdon, 1971.

Kingsbury, Jack Dean. *The Christology of Mark's Gospel.* Philadelphia: Fortress, 1983.

Kleinknecht, Karl Theodor. *Der leidende Gerechtfertigte: Die alttestamentlich-jüdische Tradition vom 'leidenden Gerechten' und ihre Rezeption bei Paulus.* WUNT 2/13. Tübingen: Mohr Siebeck, 1984.

Kümmel, Werner G. *Verheissung und Erfüllung: Untersuchungen zur eschatologischen Verkündigung Jesu.* 2d ed. Zürich: Zwingli, 1953.

Leivestad, Ragnar. *Jesus in His Own Perspective: An Examination of His Sayings, Actions, and Eschatological Titles.* Minneapolis: Augsburg, 1987.

Loader, William R. G. *The Christology of the Fourth Gospel: Structure and Issues.* BBET 23. 2d ed. Frankfurt: Lang, 1992.

Manson, T. W. *The Servant-Messiah: A Study of the Public Ministry of Jesus.* Cambridge: Cambridge University Press, 1950.

Meeks, Wayne A. *The First Urban Christians: The Social World of the Apostle Paul.* New Haven: Yale University Press, 1983.

Meier, John P. *A Marginal Jew: Rethinking the Historical Jesus.* 2 vols. New York: Doubleday, 1991-1994.

Merklein, Helmut. *Jesu Botschaft von der Gottesherrschaft.* SBS 111. 3d ed. Stuttgart: Katholisches Bibelwerk, 1989.

Moule, C. F. D. *The Origin of Christology.* Cambridge: Cambridge University Press, 1977.

Nickelsburg, George W. E., Jr. *Resurrection, Immortality, and Eternal Life in Intertestamental Judaism.* HTS 26. Cambridge: Harvard University Press, 1972.

Pokorny, Petr. *The Genesis of Christology: Foundations for a Theology of the New Testament.* Edinburgh: Clark, 1987.

Ruppert, Lothar. *Jesus als der leidende Gerechte? Der Weg Jesu im Lichte eines alt- und zwischentestamentlichen Motivs.* SBS 59. Stuttgart: Katholisches Bibelwerk, 1972.

————. *Der leidende Gerechte: Eine motivgeschichtliche Untersuchung zum Alten Testament und zwischentestamentlichen Judentum.* Forschung zur Bibel 5. Würzburg: Echter, 1973.

Sanders, E. P. *The Historical Figure of Jesus.* London: Penguin, 1993.

————. *Jesus and Judaism.* London: SCM, 1985.

Schlosser, Jacques. *Le Règne de Dieu dans les dits de Jésus.* 2 vols. Ebib. Paris: Gabalda, 1980.

Schürmann, Heinz. *Gottes Reich — Jesu Geschick: Jesu ureigener Tod im Licht seiner Basileia-Verkündigung.* Freiburg: Herder, 1983.

————. *Jesu ureigener Tod: Exegetische Besinnungen und Ausblick.* Freiburg: Herder, 1975.

Schweizer, Eduard. "Was meinen wir eigentlich wenn wir sagen 'Gott sandte seinen Sohn . . .'?" *NTS* 37 (1991) 204-24.

————. "Zum religionsgeschichtlichen Hintergrund der 'Sendungsformel' Gal 4,4f., Röm 8,3f., Joh 3,16f., 1 Joh 4,9." *ZNW* 57 (1966) 199-210.

Segal, Alan F. *Two Powers in Heaven: Early Rabbinic Reports about Christianity and Gnosticism.* SJLA 25. Leiden: Brill, 1977.

Stanton, Graham N. *The Gospels and Jesus.* Oxford: Oxford University Press, 1989.

———. *Jesus of Nazareth in New Testament Preaching.* SNTSMS 27. Cambridge: Cambridge University Press, 1974.

Steck, Odil H. *Israel und das gewaltsame Geschick der Propheten: Untersuchungen zur Überlieferung des deuteronomistischen Geschichtsbildes im Alten Testament, Spätjudentum und Urchristentum.* WMANT 23. Neukirchen-Vluyn: Neukirchener Verlag, 1967.

Taylor, Joan E. *The Immerser: John the Baptist within Second Temple Judaism.* Grand Rapids: Eerdmans, 1997.

Thüsing, Wilhelm. *Per Christum in Deum: Studien zum Verhältnis von Christozentrik und Theozentrik in den paulinischen Hauptbriefen.* NTAbh 1. 2d ed. Münster: Aschendorf, 1969.

Vermes, Geza. *Jesus the Jew: A Historian's Reading of the Gospels.* 2d ed. London: Collins, 1977.

———. *The Religion of Jesus the Jew.* London: SCM, 1993.

Williams, S. K. *Jesus' Death as Saving Event: The Background and Origin of a Concept.* HDR 2. Missoula, Mont.: Scholars Press, 1975.

For further orientation:

Chilton, Bruce, and Craig A. Evans. *Studying the Historical Jesus: Evaluation of the State of Current Research.* NTTS 19. Leiden: Brill, 1994.

Evans, Craig A. *Life of Jesus Research: An Annotated Bibliography.* NTTS 24. Rev. ed. Leiden: Brill, 1996.

Witherington, Ben III. *The Jesus Quest: The Third Search for the Jew of Nazareth.* Downers Grove, Ill.: InterVarsity, 1995.

Acknowledgments

Some of the material in this volume has been adapted from other publications by the author. The author and publisher gratefully acknowledge permission to reuse this material in this book:

"The Christological Significance of Jesus' Preaching of the Kingdom of God." In *The Future of Christology: Essays in Honor of Leander E. Keck,* edited by Abraham J. Malherbe and Wayne A. Meeks, 1-17. Minneapolis: Fortress, 1993.

"Christology and Theology in the Context of Early Christian Eschatology Particularly in the Fourth Gospel." In *The Four Gospels 1992: Festschrift Frans Neirynck,* edited by F. Van Segbroeck et al., 1835-53. BETL 100. Leuven: Leuven University Press and Peeters, 1992.

Jesus' Message about the Kingdom of God in the Light of Contemporary Ideas. The Ethel M. Wood Lecture, 1991. London: University of London, 1991.

"Jesus' Rôle in the Final Breakthrough of God's Kingdom." In *Geschichte — Tradition — Reflexion: Festschrift für Martin Hengel zum 70. Geburtstag,* edited by Hubert Cancik, Hermann Lichtenberger, and Peter Schäfer, vol. 3, 265-86. Tübingen: Mohr Siebeck, 1996.

Jesus, The Servant-Messiah. New Haven: Yale University Press, 1991.

"Mark 14:25 among Jesus' Words about the Kingdom of God." In *Sayings of Jesus, Canonical and Non-Canonical: Essays in Honour of Tjitze Baarda,* edited by William L. Petersen, Johan S. Vos, and Henk J. de Jonge, 123-35. NovTSup 89. Leiden: E. J. Brill, 1997.

"Monotheism and Christology." In *Early Christian Thought in Its Jewish Context,* edited by John Barclay and John Sweet, 225-37. Cambridge: Cambridge University Press, 1995.

Index of Names and Subjects

Index of Scripture
and Other Ancient Sources